The Approved Social Worker's Guide to Mental Health Law

Post-Qualifying Social Work Practice – titles in the series

Critical Thinking for Social Work	ISBN 13: 978 1 84445 049 7
	ISBN 10: 1 84445 049 X
Law and the Social Work Practitioner	ISBN 13: 978 1 84445 059 6
	ISBN 10: 1 84445 059 7
Vulnerable Adults and Community Care	ISBN 13: 978 1 84445 061 9
	ISBN 10: 1 84445 061 9

To order, please contact our distributor: BEBC Distribution, Albion Close, Parkstone, Poole, BH12 3LL. Telephone: 0845 230 9000, email: **learningmatters@bebc.co.uk**. You can also find more information on each of these titles and our other learning resources at **www.learningmatters.co.uk**

The Approved Social Worker's Guide to Mental Health Law

ROBERT BROWN

Series Editor: Keith Brown

LearningMatters

First published in 2006 by Learning Matters Ltd

British Library Cataloguing in Publication Data
A CIP record for this book is available from the British Library.

ISBN-10: 1 84445 062 7
ISBN-13: 978 1 84445 062 6

Cover design by Code 5 Design Associates Ltd
Project management by Deer Park Productions, Tavistock, Devon
Typeset by PDQ Typesetting Ltd
Printed and bound in Great Britain by Bell & Bain Ltd, Glasgow

Learning Matters Ltd
33 Southernhay East
Exeter EX1 1NX
Tel: 01392 215560
Email: info@learningmatters.co.uk
www.learningmatters.co.uk

Contents

Foreword to Post-Qualifying Social Work Series

All texts in the Post-Qualifying Social Work Series have been written by people with a passion for excellence in Social Work Practice. They are primarily written for Social Workers who are undertaking Post-Qualifying Social Work Awards; however they are clearly of value to any Social Worker who wants to consider up-to-date social work practice issues.

They are also of value to Social Work students as they are written to inform, inspire and develop Social Work Practice.

All the authors have a connection with the Centre for Post-Qualifying Social Work, and as a Centre we are all committed to raising the profile of the social work profession. As a Centre we trust you find this text of real value to your social work practice, and that this in turn has a real impact on the service that users and carers receive.

Keith Brown
Series Editor
Centre for Post-Qualifying Social Work

About the author

Rob Brown is Director of the Approved Social Workers Course in South West England. This is delivered in association with Bournemouth University. Rob is also the Area Mental Health Act Commissioner for Dorset and Somerset. He has been a member of the Mental Health Act Commission since 1992. Prior to that he was a Mental Welfare Officer and then an Approved Social Worker with Hampshire County Council. He has been a lecturer at Southampton University, Stirling University and Croydon College. He contributes to the training of section 12 approved doctors in South West England and provides training in mental health law. Rob has published widely in the field of mental health law.

Preface to the 2006 edition

Welcome to *The Approved Social Worker's Guide to Mental Health Law*. This has been designed primarily for those on an ASW course or for those helping to provide placement opportunities for an ASW trainee. It should also be useful for practising ASWs, other mental health professionals, service users, carers and others interested in the field of mental health law. The law covered here is that which covers England and Wales. Note that mental health law is significantly different in Scotland, in Northern Ireland and in the Channel Islands.

The Mental Health Social Work Award fits within the post-qualifying framework. Relevant competences are set out in the GSCC document Assuring Quality for Mental Health Social Work. This book cross-refers to these competences at the beginning of each chapter. Typical assignment questions and case studies are also included.

The law is changing rapidly in the mental health field. The guide is up to date as at the end of January 2006. Readers may wish to check that there has been no major recent case law which alters the position as stated here. A good source for this purpose is *www.markewalton.net*.

Recent changes which are covered in this book include:

* the Mental Capacity Act 2005
* when to consult the nearest relative (*R* v *Bristol* case [2005])
* the European Court ruling on the Bournewood case (*HL* v *UK*) and the government consultation document (2005).

The *Guide* should be read in conjunction with the Mental Health Act 1983 and the Code of Practice. Both of these are included in Jones' *Mental Health Act Manual* (9th edition 2004, Sweet & Maxwell) which is issued to most trainee ASWs.

Inevitably, there will be changes to the law during the life of this volume but we hope it will help in keeping you reasonably well informed on current mental health law. There is a list of legal references at the end of the guide and further reading at the end of each chapter.

Reforming mental health and capacity law

There is significant potential overlap between these two measures and there is some discussion on this at the end of Chapter 11. However there now also appears to be a significant gap as a result of the Bournewood case (*HL* v *UK*), where the European Court has ruled that there were breaches of Articles 5.1 and 5.4 of the European Convention on Human Rights in relation to a mentally incapacitated and compliant patient. Current law and the approach to its use were not seen as satisfying European law. This decision has both immediate and long-term implications and these are considered in Chapter 2, where there is also a description of the case itself. ASWs will need to see the Department of Health guidance (included in Appendix 2) as well as taking advice from their own legal departments.

Robert Brown
South West ASW Programme Director
c/o Institute of Health and Community Studies, Post Qualifying Social Work Team, Bournemouth University, 4th Floor, Royal London House, Christchurch Road, Bournemouth, BH1 3LT.

Chapter 1

Introduction and definitions of mental disorder

Becoming an Approved Social Worker

This chapter should help candidates to achieve the following competences:

2a Apply knowledge of mental health legislation, related codes of practice, national and local guidance.

3a Critical understanding of a range of models of mental disorder, including the contribution of social factors.

3b Critical understanding of the implications of mental disorder for service users, children, families, and carers.

Common law

Although the Approved Social Worker's (ASW's) role is rooted firmly in statute, there are frequent overlaps with the common law. The *Oxford Dictionary of Law* (2005) gives three basic definitions of common law:

- 'The part of English law based on rules developed by the royal courts during the first three centuries after the Norman Conquest (1066) as a system applicable to the whole country, as opposed to local customs'. The dictionary continues to describe the development of courts and distinguishes common law from equity.

- 'Rules of law developed by the courts as opposed to those created by statute.'

- 'A general system of law deriving exclusively from court decisions.'

Montgomery (2002) has described common law as: 'The rules which are extrapolated from the practice of the judges in deciding cases.'

Some practitioners have referred to this as 'common sense under a wig'.

An example of an area covered by common law rather than statute is treatment for mental disorder for an informal patient. Where such a patient lacks capacity they may be treated by a doctor in their best interests under the doctrine of necessity. See Chapter 6 for a more detailed discussion of this area of law.

Civil liberties *v* welfarism

Before considering models and definitions of mental disorder in depth it is important to think of the consequences which might flow from being seen as mentally disordered. This depends to some extent on the prevailing ideology as reflected in law and practice. One way of looking at the effects of different ideologies on mental health law is to contrast the views of those with 'civil libertarian' leanings such as Thomas Szasz with those of a more 'welfarist' persuasion represented by the Zito Trust. If one were to adopt Szasz's views (disputing the notion of 'mental illness' but, if conceding that it might exist, adopting the view that people should make their own decisions about their treatment, as with physical illness), then presumably there would be no need for mental health law at all. There might be a case to consider law relating to mental incapacity linked to brain injury, dementia, demonstrable learning disability, etc., but this would not allow for the detention of people who psychiatrists consider to be suffering from schizophrenia, depression, etc.

A welfarist approach might make an assumption that mental illness is linked to a degree of mental incapacity (as in the term 'lack of insight') but whether or not this is the case, a welfarist view would be that it is sometimes necessary to intervene against someone's will to protect a person from themselves or for the protection of others.

The contrast between these competing ideologies is illustrated in Figure 1.1. The Mental Health Act 1983 can be seen as positioned somewhere in the middle of the upper continuum illustrated. ASWs, doctors, tribunals and courts are left to make decisions as to when the circumstances justify intervention. With the exception of the Court of Protection, however, mental capacity is not the relevant test used in the Act. The criteria needed are a mental disorder of a nature or degree to warrant intervention plus an appropriate level of risk.

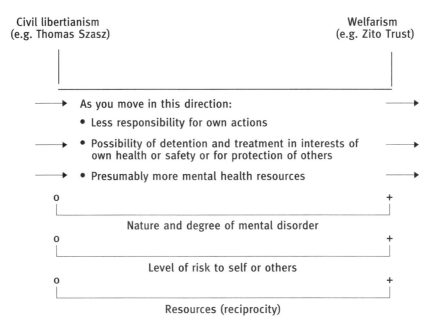

Figure 1.1 Diagram to illustrate different perspectives on mental health law

Gostin (1975) made the ethical point that, if you deprive someone of liberty, you should have a duty to provide a good quality service. One part of the Mental Health Act which addresses this issue is section 117 relating to after-care. Recent guidance that section 117 services should not incur charges could be seen to reflect the link between the positive end of the resource continuum with the welfarist intervention point. Similarly, the Richardson Committee on the Reform of Mental Health Act considered the principle of 'reciprocity' (see Chapter 11). The government's proposals in the Draft Mental Health Bill would allow charges for a number of services, including after-care, except for those people subject to some form of compulsion at the relevant time.

Another way of using the diagram above is to imagine a point in the middle of the upper continuum where detention would be justified if there was:

- mental disorder of a nature or degree to justify this, and
- a level of risk to self or others which also justified detention.

Mental health terminology and the law

Common law distinguished 'idiots' from 'lunatics' before the first of the Acts. These terms correspond with the distinction between people with a learning disability and those who are mentally ill. Historically, the groups have sometimes been dealt with in separate legislation and sometimes together, as in the Mental Health Act 1983.

1713/1744 Vagrancy Acts allowed detention of 'Lunaticks or mad persons'.

1774 Act for regulating private madhouses.

1845 Lunatics Act included 'Person of unsound mind'.

1886 Idiots Act provided separately for idiots and imbeciles.

1890 Lunacy (Consolidation) Act ignored the distinction.

1913 Mental Deficiency Act favoured segregation of 'mental defectives': *idiots* unable to guard themselves against common physical dangers such as fire, water or traffic; *imbeciles* could guard against physical dangers but were incapable of managing themselves or their affairs; *feeble-minded* needed care or control for protection of self or others; *moral defectives* had vicious or criminal propensities (use of this category later included many poor women with unsupported babies).

1927 Mental Deficiency Act emphasised care outside institutions. Mental deficiency was defined as 'a condition of arrested or incomplete development of mind existing before the age of 18 years whether arising from inherent causes or induced by disease or injury'.

1930 Mental Treatment Act allowed for voluntary admissions.

1946 NHS Act – ended distinction between paying and non-paying patients.

1948 National Assistance Act – made provisions for those in need.

1959 Mental Health Act. Mental disorder means: 'mental illness; arrested or incomplete development of mind, psychopathic disorder, and any other disorder or disability of mind'. Further classifications for long-term compulsion were: mental illness, severe subnormality; subnormality; psychopathic disorder with a kind of treatability test for the last two.

1970 LA Social Services Act created Social Services Departments.

1983   Mental Health Act. The broad definition is exactly the same as in the 1959 Act. However, the classifications changed to: *mental illness* (undefined): *severe mental impairment:* 'a state of arrested or incomplete development of mind which includes severe impairment of intelligence and social functioning and is associated with abnormally aggressive or seriously irresponsible conduct on the part of the person concerned'; *mental impairment:* 'a state of arrested or incomplete development of mind (not amounting to severe mental impairment) which includes significant impairment of intelligence and social functioning and is associated with abnormally aggressive or seriously irresponsible conduct on the part of the person concerned'; *psychopathic disorder:* 'a persistent disorder or disability of mind (whether or not including significant impairment of intelligence) which results in abnormally aggressive or seriously irresponsible conduct on the part of the person concerned'.

1984   Police and Criminal Evidence Act (and its Codes of Practice) uses the term 'mental disorder' as per the Mental Health Act and the revised PACE Codes (2004) use the concept of the mentally vulnerable adult.

2002   Draft Mental Health Bill definition: 'any disability or disorder of mind or brain which results in an impairment or disturbance of mental functioning'.

2003   Mental Capacity Bill – people unable to make a decision 'because of an impairment of, or a disturbance in the functioning of, the mind or brain'.

2004   Revised Draft Mental Health Bill definition of mental disorder is: 'an impairment of or a disturbance in the functioning of mind or brain resulting from any disability or disorder of the mind or brain'.

2005   Parliamentary Scrutiny Committee accept the above definition but state: 'that a broad definition of mental disorder in the draft Bill must be accompanied by explicit and specific exclusions which safeguard against the legislation being used inappropriately as a means of social control'.

The Scottish Mental Health Act 2003 defines mental disorder as mental illness, personality disorder or learning disability. This is probably more in line with current mental health practice than the proposed definition for England and Wales.

Models of mental disorder

There are many theoretical approaches to mental disorder. In the *Journal of Mental Health* Pilgrim (2002) traces the history of the biopsychosocial model. There is also a chapter by Dallos in the Open University text, *Mental Health Matters* (1996). This is rather light on social explanations so the following paragraphs outline the bio-social model and look at a few other approaches. Dallos identified three levels of analysis: societal, interpersonal or individual. He described what he saw as the most influential psychological frameworks under these headings: biological and medical, behavioural, psychodynamic, humanistic and systemic. They share important features (e.g. in terms of the importance of empathy, the therapeutic relationship and clear communication) but they can lead to different approaches to intervention.

Biological and medical frameworks

These would see problems stemming from physical causes including illness, accident and hereditary factors. Some theorists suggest that schizophrenia and depression are linked to brain defects such as neurotransmitter problems. Medical frameworks see mental health problems as similar to physical illness. This leads to classification of mental disorders and a regime of treatment which relies heavily on the use of medication. Psycho-education approaches often have a biological view of causation but also recognise that, as with physical illness, social and environmental factors interact with the illness. Some approaches emphasise the importance of stress and lead to treatments which include work with the emotional atmosphere in families (see Leff and Vaughn, 1985).

Behavioural frameworks

These suggest psychological problems are acquired through learning experiences and then affected by various punishments and rewards from social interaction. Treatments might include systematic desensitisation (e.g. with phobias), behaviour modification (e.g. to remove rewards which are maintaining problem behaviour) or cognitive-behavioural approaches (which would include helping people to modify immediate cognitive response to potentially upsetting situations). Cognitive-behavioural techniques have recently gained some ground within psychiatric practice in Britain.

Psychodynamic approaches

An individual's emotional experiences (especially in early childhood) are seen as the primary cause of later problems. Treatment often focuses on bringing memories of these early experiences into consciousness and thereby enabling the person to deal with them in a way that empowers them to be more autonomous. Some theorists (such as Freud) emphasised the importance of sexuality and an inability to resolve sexual feelings within a family. Treatment often focuses on the therapeutic relationship and the concept of transference (e.g. the patient transfers feelings from earlier relationships on to the therapist). Psychoanalysis is an expensive and time-intensive therapy but briefer psychodynamic techniques have also been developed.

Humanistic frameworks

These also consider unconscious processes but see people as essentially creative and motivated by a need to grow and develop. Conscious and unconscious states can be integrated. leading to more autonomy and freedom. Use is made of art, music, writing, drama, etc. The emphasis is on self-direction rather than interpretation and may lead to support groups being formed or self-help groups with no therapist involvement.

Systemic frameworks

These see problems as being rooted in communications within relationships and in patterns of action rather than within the individual. Systemic family therapy focuses on communication within the family and uses feedback to look at how people's actions relate to the effects of previous actions. Repetitive relationships patterns are seen to arise partly from shared beliefs and understandings.

Social Models

There are various versions of a social model of mental disorder. At one level, mental illness would be seen as a consequence of social disadvantage, the symptom of a sick society. The solution would lie in improving social and physical conditions. In 1992 David Goldberg and Peter Huxley published an influential text entitled *Common Mental Disorders: A Bio-Social model*, which sought to link some social factors in mental disorder with biological aspects.

Their model looks at susceptibility to mental disorder in terms of social, psychological and biological factors. Their work is based on three key concepts:

- vulnerability – factors which make some people more susceptible to episodes of mental disorder; a vulnerable individual may experience symptoms after a relatively minor stress
- destabilisation – the process of beginning to experience symptoms
- restitution – the process of losing symptoms; factors which determine how long an episode of illness will last in a given individual.

In summarising key features of the model, Goldberg and Huxley (1992, p. 144) state:

> *The development of different types of symptom is seen as being determined by early childhood events, the present social circumstances and the kind of provoking event, and not at all by genetic factors. Genetic factors are seen as being very important in determining overall vulnerability towards common mental disorders and are responsible for some of the specific vulnerability to major mental disorders such as schizophrenia and bipolar illness, but they do not determine why one person will become depressed and another anxious.*

Another helpful text which gives some different perspectives on mental disorder is *Mental Health in a Multi-ethnic Society* edited by Suman Fernando (1995).

Other models

Historically and culturally there have been wide-ranging explanations for mental disorder. Some of those not included above are:

- *The moral model.* The person's behaviour is seen as bad on the basis of judgements made on their observed behaviour and they need moral treatment.
- *The impaired model.* The person is seen as handicapped and unlikely to be restored to normality by treatment.
- *The psychedelic model.* The mad have been chosen by society to act out its problems. They can reveal themselves as particularly gifted members of society and must be allowed to develop their potential for inner exploration and to change the world through their insights.
- *The conspiratorial model.* Madness stems from the way mentally ill people are labelled. See the work of Thomas Scheff, Szasz and Laing.

Models of mental disorder and the law

People's understanding of how the mind works, together with their views on mental capacity, free will, determinism and social responsibility, combine to influence how they think the law should operate in this field. The Mental Health Act 1983 and proposals for legal change make assumptions and reflect some models of mental disorder more strongly than others. It helps to have a grasp of these models in order to consider how the law will affect service users and carers and how it might constrain their ability to choose an approach that matches their own preferred explanations.

Definitions of mental disorder (section 1)

Introduction

Definitions of mental disorder are of central importance as the Act only applies to those believed to be mentally disordered. Section 1 states: 'The provisions of this Act shall have effect with respect to the reception, care and treatment of mentally disordered patients, the management of their property and other related matters.' Judgements on mental disorder may be made by a range of people, e.g. doctors, police, magistrates, Mental Health Review Tribunal members. In each case, judgements must be made within the framework of the definitions given in section 1. Coming within the definition of mental disorder is not sufficient, by itself, to warrant detention in hospital. The disorder must be of a nature or degree to warrant detention. Unless the person is seen as mentally disordered, the Act does not apply. Problems of including people with learning disabilities are considered below under 'Discussion'.

The 2004 Draft Mental Health Bill includes a broad definition of mental disorder. It would be seen as 'an impairment of or a disturbance in the functioning of mind or brain resulting from any disability or disorder of the mind or brain'. If this broad definition were to be adopted, some of the problems discussed below in relation to classifications of mental disorder might be avoided, but new problems might emerge.

Broad definition of 'mental disorder'

The Mental Health Act 1983 gives a broad definition of the generic term 'mental disorder' and then four specific classifications which will be considered below: mental illness, severe mental impairment, mental impairment, psychopathic disorder. Mental disorder is described in section 1(2) as: 'mental illness, arrested or incomplete development of mind, psychopathic disorder and any other disorder or disability of mind'.

It is the relevant definition for the following sections:

s2 admission for assessment
s4 admission in cases of emergency
s5(2) Doctor's holding power
s5(4) Nurse's holding power
s131 informal admission
s135 warrant to search for and remove patients
s136 Police powers to remove persons from public places.

Mental illness is discussed in more detail below.

'Arrested or incomplete development of mind' would cover a number of people with significant learning disabilities. The guidance given in para. 30.5 of the Code of Practice (DoH, 1999) states:

> *This implies that the features that determine the learning disability were present at some stage which permanently prevented the usual maturation of intellectual and social development. It excludes persons whose learning disability derives from accident, injury or illness occurring after that point usually accepted as complete development.*

There is no age specified, but clearly, if the cause of the mental disability was an accident to an adult, they would be excluded from this definition. Note that this would also exclude the person from the definitions of mental impairment and severe mental impairment given below. This would be a problem where such a person needed long-term detention or guardianship. Again, this issue is dealt with in the paragraphs headed 'Discussion'. Such a person, however, could be included under: 'Any other disorder or disability of mind'. This would cover a number of conditions and would depend to some extent on how broad a definition of mental illness is used. It could include mental disabilities arising from accidents or illness, including the after effects of mental illness.

Specific classifications of 'mental disorder'

A patient must be considered to be suffering from one of the four specific forms of mental disorder (mental illness, severe mental impairment, mental impairment or psychopathic disorder) before they can be dealt with under the following sections:

s3 admission for treatment
s7 reception into guardianship
s25A supervised after-care
s35 remand to hospital for report on accused's mental condition
s36 remand to hospital for treatment (mental illness or severe mental impairment)
s37 court order for hospital admission or guardianship
s38 interim hospital order
s45A hospital direction (psychopathic disorder)
s47 transfer to hospital of people serving prison sentences
s48 transfer to hospital of other prisoners (mental illness, severe mental impairment).

'Mental illness' is not defined in the Act. The search for an acceptable definition was given up on the grounds that the lack of a definition in the 1959 Act had not caused any difficulties in practice. Lawton LJ endorsed this view in a Court of Appeal case. He adopted a lay view of mental illness in his response to a man (who amongst other things had put his cat in a gas oven, cut its throat, hanged a puppy, and pushed his wife downstairs as a way of getting rid of the baby she was expecting) with this statement:

> *I ask myself, what would the ordinary sensible person have said about the patient's condition in this case if he has been informed of his behaviour to the dogs, the cat and his wife? In my judgement such a person would have said, 'Well, the fellow is obviously mentally ill.'*

This has become known as 'the-man-must-be-mad' test. However, Hoggett (1996, p.32) has pointed to the problems in this approach from a consumer viewpoint. Without a definition in statute, it falls to professionals to provide one but this could be oppressive and is open to abuse. There are useful guidelines elsewhere. The Butler Report (1975) considered mental illness to be a 'a disorder which has not always existed in the patient but has developed as a condition overlying the sufferer's usual personality'.

A Review of the Mental Health Act 1959 (1976) states:

> *Mental illness means an illness having one or more of the following characteristics:*
> *(i) More than temporary impairment of intellectual functions shown by a failure of memory, orientation, comprehension and learning capacity*

> *(ii) More than temporary alteration of mood of such degree as to give rise to the patient having a delusional appraisal of his situation, his past or his future, or that of others or to the lack of any appraisal*
> *(iii) Delusional beliefs, persecutory, jealous or grandiose*
> *(iv) Abnormal perceptions associated with delusional misinterpretation of events*
> *(v) Thinking so disordered as to prevent the patient making a reasonable appraisal of his situation or having reasonable communication with others.*

In the Mental Health (Northern Ireland) Order 1986 mental illness is defined as a 'state of mind which affects a person's thinking, perceiving, emotion or judgement to the extent that he requires care or medical treatment in his own interests or in the interest of other persons'.

In practice, mental illness is seen as including psychotic states, major disorders such as schizophrenia, serious mood disorders, anorexia nervosa and dementia. Some professionals are guided by the views expressed above. There is, however, a variation in the use of the term 'mental illness'.

Paragraph 8 of the Memorandum to the Mental Health Act states that the 'operational definition and usage is a matter for clinical judgement in each case'.

'Severe mental impairment' is defined in section 1(2) as: 'a state of arrested or incomplete development of mind which includes severe impairment of intelligence and social functioning and is associated with abnormally aggressive or seriously irresponsible conduct on the part of the person concerned'.

'Mental impairment' is defined in section 1(2) as: 'a state of arrested or incomplete development of mind (not amounting to severe mental impairment) which includes significant impairment of intelligence and social functioning and is associated with abnormally aggressive or seriously irresponsible conduct on the part of the person concerned.'

The Code of Practice offers guidance to understanding the terms used and how to determine severity. It emphasises the need for reliable and careful assessment and notes in para 30.5:

> Severe or significant impairment of social functioning. *The evidence of the degree and nature of social competence should be based on reliable and recent observations, preferably from a number of sources such as social workers, nurses and psychologists. Such evidence should include the result of one or more social functioning assessment tests.*
>
> Abnormally aggressive behaviour. *Any assessment of this category should be based on observations of behaviour which lead to a conclusion that the actions are outside the usual range of aggressive behaviour, and which cause actual damage and/or real distress occurring recently or persistently or with excessive severity.*
>
> Irresponsible conduct. *The assessment of this characteristic should be based on an observation of behaviour which shows a lack of responsibility, a disregard of the consequences of action taken, and where the results cause actual damage or real distress, either recently or persistently or with excessive severity.*

The Act's use of the word 'impairment' could be criticised. The word had previously been used to mean loss or absence of function but is now associated with the idea of someone whose behaviour is abnormally aggressive or seriously irresponsible. The rationale behind the change was that a small minority of people with arrested or incomplete development of mind might need longer-term detention, and that the crucial determining factors would be the presence of abnormally aggressive or seriously irresponsible conduct. Similarly, there are critics of the Code of Practice's broad interpretation of irresponsible conduct and queries whether this covers those unable to protect themselves from abuse or exploitation (see Discussion below).

'Psychopathic disorder' is defined as: 'a persistent disorder or disability of mind (whether or not including significant impairment of intelligence) which results in abnormally aggressive or seriously irresponsible conduct on the part of the person concerned'. The Butler Committee (1975) concluded that it was no longer a useful or meaningful concept, but it survived in the 1983 Act. The key elements in the definition are persistence and that the abnormally aggressive or seriously irresponsible conduct results from the condition.

Discussion

It should be noted that there was a school of thought which said that people with learning disabilities should be excluded from this legislation. Some groups thought that they should either be dealt with under separate legislation or should not be subject to any form of compulsion. The counter view was that people with learning disabilities should be included, with 'mental handicap' being identified as a classification of mental disorder. The compromise position adopted in the Act was that at least a minority of such people should be covered by the Mental Health Act in general, and that an even smaller group, who were abnormally aggressive or seriously irresponsible, should be liable to longer-term compulsion in some circumstances. There was some confusion generated by this compromise. Even after publication in 1983, some people believed the Act stated that people with learning disabilities could only be detained if they were also abnormally aggressive or seriously irresponsible. It has been seen above that, in fact, this restriction only applies to some sections (e.g. ss 3, 7 and 37). The more general definition of 'arrested or incomplete development of mind' would be enough to meet the requirements of section 2 as this is included in the broad definition of mental disorder. A look at the Parliamentary Scrutiny Committee report (p. 33) shows that confusion still exists, as their explanation of the current law contains errors, e.g. stating that arrested or incomplete development of mind must be associated with abnormally aggressive or seriously irresponsible conduct before someone can be detained on section 2.

One by-product of the compromise in the 1983 Act has been the exclusion of some people from the provisions of guardianship where they might have benefited from it. These are people who have suffered arrested or incomplete development of mind, who are subject to exploitation or neglect, but would not be seen as abnormally aggressive or seriously irresponsible, thereby excluding them from the definition of mental impairment. Apart from a change in state, the only way such individuals may be received into guardianship is where the relevant professionals take a liberal interpretation of the Code of Practice definition in para. 30.5 as discussed above. Some doctors and others have, understandably, not been willing to see someone who is exploited or neglected as 'seriously irresponsible' just because they have failed to rectify the position for themselves. The death due to parental neglect of Beverley Lewis in 1989 drew this problem to people's attention. In a recent Court of Appeal case [30.9.1999 – In *re F (a child) (Care order: Sexual abuse)*] judges overturned a County Court Judge's view (when displacing her father as nearest relative) that a 17-year-old with learning disability who wished to return home where she would be at risk of abuse was acting in a 'seriously irresponsible' manner. The

Appeal Court preferred a more restrictive interpretation of this phrase. Subsequent court decisions have followed this line.

The exclusion of adults who sustain head injuries is a further problem. Except in cases resulting in behaviour which a doctor can describe as mental illness (as has sometimes been the case with frontal lobe damage), such people can only be detained under section 2. They could not be detained under section 3, or received into guardianship under section 7, because they only fit the definition of 'any other disorder or disability of mind' coming within the general definition of 'mental disorder'.

In a follow-up to *Re F*, the Court held that the common law doctrine of necessity is not limited to medical matters. The High Court may therefore be prepared to intervene in some cases where guardianship is precluded because of the definition problem. In *Re. S* (2002) EWHC 2278 (Fam) the Court confirmed that in certain circumstances a local authority might intervene in the best interests of a mentally incapacitated adult against the wishes of other family members. In some situations this might require an application to the High Court for declaratory relief.

The 'treatability test'

The Mental Health Act 1959 had four classifications of mental disorder: mental illness, severe subnormality, subnormality and psychopathic disorder. The last two were seen as less serious than the first two and likely to ease with the maturity of the individual. Consequently, it was not possible to compulsorily admit a 'subnormal' or 'psychopathic patient' after the age of 21 or to renew their detention beyond the age of 25. The definitions of these two terms also included the idea of susceptibility to medical treatment. The 1983 Act dropped the age requirements but replaced them with what is referred to as 'the treatability test', which applies to the two less serious conditions of mental impairment and psychopathic disorder. Thus, to detain a 'mentally impaired' or 'psychopathic' patient under section 3, treatment must be 'likely to alleviate or prevent a deterioration' in the patient's condition. There should be a strong possibility that the disorder will be affected by treatment but not necessarily an expectation of a 'cure'.

'Mental illness' and 'severe mental impairment' were seen as more serious conditions which might sometimes require detention of the patient in a crisis even when the condition might not respond to treatment. In order to renew the detention of a mentally ill or severely mentally impaired patient, however, section 20 requires that the responsible medical officer must certify either that 'treatment is likely to alleviate or prevent a deterioration of his condition' or 'that the patient, if discharged, is unlikely to be able to care for himself, to obtain the care which he needs or to guard himself against serious exploitation'.

Medical treatment itself is defined in section 145 of the Mental Health Act 1983; it includes nursing, and also includes 'care, habilitation and rehabilitation under medical supervision'. This is a very broad concept and would cover most aspects of patient management carried out under medical supervision. Para. 15.4 of the Code of Practice states that the s145 definition of medical treatment constitutes: 'the broad range of activities aimed at alleviating, or preventing a deterioration of the patient's mental disorder. It includes physical treatment such as ECT and the administration of drugs, and psychotherapy'. See Chapter 6 for a flowchart on consent to treatment decisions.

Exclusions

Section 1(3) excludes certain behaviours from being seen in themselves as mental disorders: 'promiscuity or other immoral conduct, sexual deviancy or dependence on alcohol or drugs'. They may, however, be associated with or lead to mental disorder and thereby become relevant considerations. The DHSS, in *Review of the Mental Health Act 1959* (1978) saw these as 'social and behavioural problems' rather than mental disorders. The Draft Bill has no exclusions, which has led to concerns about mental health law being used to control social problems. See discussion in Chapter 11. In general, Hoggett (1996) argues that the distinction in law between social or behavioural problems on the one hand and mental disorder on the other is still far from clear. The current discussions on how to deal with people who have a severe personality disorder are a good illustration of her argument. While we await new legislation we are left with the interpretations of the expression 'mental disorder' which doctors, police officers, tribunals, the courts and others choose to adopt.

Two graphical illustrations of section 1 are given in the box below and in Figure 1.2 for guidance:

Summary of 'mental disorder' as defined in section 1 of the Mental Health Act 1983

(1) MENTAL ILLNESS	} one of these is
(2) SEVERE MENTAL IMPAIRMENT	needed for a

——————— *treatability test* for s3 and s37* ———

(3) MENTAL IMPAIRMENT**	} section 3, 37 or
(4) PSYCHOPATHIC DISORDER	s7 (guardianship)

5) arrested or incomplete development of mind	} OK for sections
6) any other disorder or disability of mind.	2, 4, 5, 135, 136

But a person should not be seen as suffering from a mental disorder by reason only of:

- promiscuity or other immoral conduct,
- sexual deviancy,
- dependence on alcohol or drugs.

* *the treatability test requires that medical treatment in a hospital is likely to alleviate or prevent a deterioration of the patient's condition*

** *Mental impairment = a state of arrested or incomplete development of mind which includes significant impairment of intelligence and social functioning and is associated with abnormally aggressive or seriously irresponsible conduct on the part of the person concerned.*

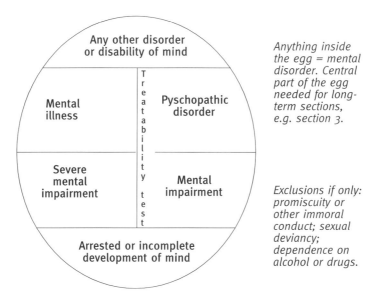

Anything inside the egg = mental disorder. Central part of the egg needed for long-term sections, e.g. section 3.

Exclusions if only: promiscuity or other immoral conduct; sexual deviancy; dependence on alcohol or drugs.

Figure 1.2 'Nancy's egg' – Mental Disorder as defined in s1 Mental Health Act 1983
(from an idea by Nancy Atkinson)

Activity **1.1**

Sample questions on definitions
(questions are typical ASW examination questions and are usually in three parts)

1a What may be included as forms of mental disorder as per section 1 of the Mental Health Act 1983 when considering a possible compulsory admission under section 2? (Do not go into any details on definitions of terms used.)

*1b List the forms of behaviour which, by themselves, are **excluded** from being a mental disorder under section 1.*

1c Using one as an example, identify why an exclusion may be a problem for those considering the use of section 2.

2a What are the essential elements of the definition of 'psychopathic disorder' (as given in section 1 of the Mental Health Act 1983)?

2b What is the 'treatability test' and when does it come into effect?

2c Why, in social policy terms, is treatability such a big issue currently in relation to psychopathic disorder?

Chapter 2
Civil admissions, guardianship and supervised after-care

Periods of compulsion, access to Mental Health Review Tribunals (MRTs) and consent to treatment for patients covered by Part II of the Mental Health Act 1983

Section number and purpose	Maximum duration	Can patient apply to MHRT?	Can nearest relative apply to MHRT?	Will there be an automatic MHRT hearing?	Do consent to treatment rules apply?
2 Admission for assessment	**28 days** Not renewable	Within first 14 days	No – s23 gives discharge power; but see s25	No	Yes
3 Admission for treatment	**6 months** May be renewed for 6 months and then yearly	Within first 6 months and then in each period	No – s23 gives discharge power; but see s25	Yes – at 6 months and then every 3 years (yearly if under 16) if no application	Yes
4 Admission for assessment in an emergency	**72 hours** Not renewable but second doctor can change to s2	Yes. But only relevant if s4 is converted to s2	No	No	No
5(2) Doctor's holding power	**72 hours** Not renewable	No	No	No	No

Section number and purpose	Maximum duration	Can patient apply to MHRT?	Can nearest relative apply to MHRT?	Will there be an automatic MHRT hearing?	Do consent to treatment rules apply?
5(4) Nurse's holding power	**6 hours** – not renewable but doctor can change to 5(2)	No	No	No	No
7 Reception into Guardianship	**6 months** May be renewed for 6 months and then yearly	Within first 6 months and then in each period	No – s23 gives them power to discharge	No	No
16 Doctor reclassifies the mental disorder	For the duration of the detention	Within 28 days of being informed	Within 28 days of being informed	No	–
19 Transfer from guardianship to hospital	**6 months** May be renewed for 6 months and then yearly	In first 6 months of detention and then in each period	No – s23 gives them power to discharge; but see s25	Yes – at 6 months every 3 years (yearly if under 16 if no application)	Yes
25 Restriction of discharge by nearest relative	Variable	No	Within 28 days of being informed (no appeal if s2)	No	–
25A Supervised aftercare	**6 months** May be renewed for 6 months and then yearly	Within first 6 months and then in each period	Yes, if entitled to be informed, once in each period	No	No
29 Appointment of acting nearest relative by court	Variable	No	Within one year and then yearly	No	No
135 Warrant to search for and remove patient	**72 hours** Not renewable	No	No	No	No
136 Police power in public places	**72 hours** Not renewable	No	No	No	No

Compulsory admission to hospital and detention under sections 2, 3, 4, 5 or 135 of the Mental Health Act 1983

Introduction

This chapter concentrates on civil admissions (as opposed to those involving the courts – see Chapter 5). There are variations in the criteria for admissions to hospital between the different sections and these are set out below. Before looking at each of the sections in turn, however, it should be stressed that the need for the ASW to seek the 'least restrictive alternative' is common to all of them (see Chapter 4). Careful attention should be paid to the grounds for detention. In practice, the expression 'a danger to himself or others' is often used erroneously for section 2 in place of the actual grounds, i.e. that detention is necessary for the patient 'in the interests of his own health or safety or with a view to the protection of other persons'. The 'danger' grounds only come into play where the nearest relative intends to discharge the patient (see the last paragraph on section 2 below beginning 'Section 11(3)').

Similarly, mistakes are made by people not concentrating on whether it is an 'or' or an 'and' in the text. Note, for example, that it could be either the nature or degree of mental disorder which makes an admission appropriate. Again, an admission may be necessary for the health or safety of the patient or with a view to the protection of others. All three conditions do not need to be met, so health grounds alone could suffice. In contrast, note the importance of the and between 2(2)(a) and (b) below. The requirements of (a) and (b) must be met before detention is possible.

Section 131 promotes the use of informal admission wherever possible. The philosophy of the Act is to seek the least restrictive alternative and this should be borne in mind when considering the use of any of the following sections. However, note the potential effect of the European Court's decision in *HL* v *UK* (Bournewood case) described after the notes on section 5 later in this part of the chapter.

Admission for assessment – section 2

Section 2 allows for a patient who meets certain criteria to be compulsorily admitted to hospital and to be detained there for up to 28 days. The admission is for assessment (or for assessment followed by medical treatment) rather than for observation as was the case with the 1959 Act, because, in the words of the 1981 White Paper: 'it implies more active intervention to form a diagnosis and to plan treatment' (DHSS, 1981).

Two doctors need to sign recommendations (singly or jointly) based on their examinations of the patient. Section 12 requires at least one doctor to have special experience in the diagnosis or treatment of mental disorder and one should preferably have previous acquaintance with the patient. What amounts to 'previous acquaintance' was dealt with in *Reed (Trainer) v Bronglais Hospital* (2001). Here the doctor in question:

- attended a case conference which gave much background information on the patient and included the minutes of two previous case conferences
- following the case conference, saw the patient for about 5 minutes
- 'scanned' the medical records received from the Family Health Authority

- then saw the patient again to make his recommendation.

The Court held that the words should be given their ordinary meaning and that the reference in the Code to 'personal' knowledge did not import any greater requirement. The doctor had sufficient 'previous acquaintance', and any doctor would have who had some previous knowledge of the patient and was not coming to him or her 'cold'.

The recommendations will state as per section 2(2):

(a) he is suffering from mental disorder of a nature or degree which warrants the detention of the patient in a hospital for assessment (or for assessment followed by medical treatment) for at least a limited period; and

(b) he ought to be so detained in the interests of his own health or safety or with a view to the protection of other persons.

An application to hospital must be based on these two medical recommendations and may be made by either an ASW or the patient's nearest relative. The Code of Practice states:

> 2.35 *The ASW is usually the right applicant, bearing in mind professional training, knowledge of the legislation and of local resources, together with the potentially adverse effect that an application by the nearest relative might have on the latter's relationship with the patient. The doctor should therefore advise the nearest relative that it is preferable for an ASW to make an assessment of the need for a patient to be admitted under the Act, and for the ASW to make the application. When reasonably practicable the doctor should, however, advise the nearest relative of the rights set out in section 13(4) ... and of his or her right to make an application.*
> 2.36 *The doctor should never advise the nearest relative to make the application in order to avoid involving an ASW in an assessment.*

There has been some debate concerning the nearest relative as applicant. Para. 2.32 of the Code of Practice indicates that where the ASW decides not to make an application they should inform the nearest relative of their own right to make an application. They should advise the nearest relative to consult with the doctors if they wish to pursue this option. This might, however, involve a professional disagreement between the ASW and the doctors (see paras. 2.33–2.34 for advice on how to resolve this). It would probably be good practice for an ASW to explain these rights as early as possible in the assessment process. It might cause some confusion and difficulty if this were left until the last moment in a case where the ASW had decided not to make an application.

Where the nearest relative is the applicant, section 14 requires a social worker to provide a social circumstances report to the hospital. If this social worker happens to be an ASW who has earlier refused to make an application, Richard Jones (2004, p.101) is of the opinion that the report should 'include an account of the reasons for his decision.' Presumably, in cases where an ASW thought that compulsory admission was inappropriate they would already have made these reasons clear to the nearest relative and to the doctors involved and possibly to the hospital managers. The Code of Practice states:

> 11.8 *If an ASW is the applicant, he or she has a professional responsibility for ensuring that all the necessary arrangements are made for the patient to be conveyed to hospital.*

> 11.9 *If the nearest relative is the applicant, the assistance of an ASW should be made available if requested. If this is not possible, other professionals involved in the admission should give advice and assistance.*

Section 11(3) requires the ASW, when applying for a section 2 detention, to inform the nearest relative of their rights to discharge the patient under section 23. This, together with section 25, allows the nearest relative to discharge the patient if they have given 72 hours' written notice to the hospital managers of their intention to discharge the patient. The responsible medical officer (RMO) may only block this if able to produce within the 72 hours 'a report certifying that, in the opinion of that officer, the patient, if discharged, would be likely to act in a manner dangerous to other persons or to himself'. (See the chart of risk criteria in the section 'Two-stage approach to a Mental Health Act assessment'.)

Admission for treatment – section 3

This allows a patient to be compulsorily admitted to hospital and detained there for up to six months in the first instance. If the grounds are still met, detention may be renewed for six months and after that for a year at a time. The process involves the RMO examining the patient within the last two months of the period of detention and submitting a report to the hospital managers. If the patient has not had an MHRT hearing during the first six months, there will be an automatic one if detention is renewed. The admission is for treatment and two doctors sign recommendations (singly or jointly) based on their examinations of the patient. As with section 2, at least one doctor must be approved under section 12 and one should preferably have previous acquaintance with the patient. The recommendations will state that:

- he is suffering from mental illness, severe mental impairment, psychopathic disorder or mental impairment and his mental disorder is of a nature or degree which makes it appropriate for him to receive medical treatment in a hospital

- in the case of psychopathic disorder or mental impairment, such treatment is likely to alleviate or prevent a deterioration of his condition

- it is necessary for the health or safety of the patient or for the protection of other persons that he should receive such treatment and it cannot be provided unless he is detained under this section.

An application to a hospital must be based on these medical recommendations and may be made by either an ASW or the patient's nearest relative. If the ASW intends to apply, they must contact the nearest relative unless this is not reasonably practicable or would involve unreasonable delay. If the nearest relative objects to the application, it may not be made. If the ASW thinks the nearest relative is acting unreasonably they may make an application to the County Court under section 29 for the displacement of the nearest relative. It would be unusual not to be able to contact the nearest relative for s3 unless the ASW was unable to trace where they were. Para. 2.16 of the Code of Practice states:

> *If the ASW has been unable to consult the nearest relative before making an application for admission for treatment ... he or she should persist in seeking to contact the nearest relative so as to inform the latter of his or her powers to discharge the patient under section 23. The ASW should inform the hospital as soon as this has been done.*

Chapter 3 of this guide includes further discussion on nearest relative issues including the impact of the Bristol case on what is 'reasonably practical'.

The choice between section 2 and section 3

This is a matter for professional judgement of the criteria involved. Para. 5.2 of the Code of Practice gives six pointers to when section 2 might be appropriate:

a. the diagnosis and prognosis of a patient's condition is unclear

b. a need to carry out an in-patient assessment in order to formulate a treatment plan

c. a judgement is needed as to whether the patient will accept treatment on a voluntary basis following admission

d. a judgement has to be made as to whether a particular treatment proposal, which can only be administered to the patient under Part IV of the Act, is likely to be effective

e. the condition of a patient who has already been assessed, and who has been previously admitted compulsorily under the Act, is judged to have changed since the previous admission and further assessment is needed

f. the patient has not previously been admitted to hospital either compulsorily or informally and has not been in regular contact with the specialist psychiatric services.

Para. 5.3 gives two pointers where section 3 might be indicated:

a. The patient is considered to need compulsory admission for the treatment of a mental disorder which is already known to his clinical team, and has been assessed in the recent past by that team. In these circumstances, it may be right to use section 3 even where the patient has not previously been admitted as an in-patient.

b. The patient is detained under section 2 and assessment indicates a need for treatment under the Act for a period beyond the 28 day detention under section 2. In such circumstances an application for detention under section 3 should be made at the earliest opportunity and should not be delayed until the end of section 2 detention. The change in detention status from section 2 to section 3 will not deprive the patient of a Mental Health Review Tribunal hearing if the change takes place after a valid application has been made to the Tribunal but before that application has been heard. The patient's rights to apply for a Tribunal under s66(b) in the first period of detention after his change of status are unaffected.

Para. 5.4 states that decisions should not be influenced by the possibility that:

a. proposed treatment to be administered under the Act will last less than 28 days

b. a patient detained under section 2 will get quicker access to a Mental Health Review Tribunal than one detained under section 3

c. after-care under supervision will only be available if the patient has been admitted under section 3 the use of section 3 ... must be justified by the patient's need to be admitted for treatment under the terms of that section, not considerations about what is to happen after his or her eventual discharge

d. a patient's nearest relative objects to admission under section 3.

Para. 5.5 notes that 'further section 2 application cannot be made if the patient is already in hospital following admission under section 2' (reference is to *R v Wilson ex parte W* [1996]). Where a decision has been made that the primary purpose of the admission is for treatment and where the description given under 5.3a of the Code is not balanced by pointers under 5.2, there can be problems where the nearest relative objects to a section 3 and where the patient is in the community and the situation is seen as high risk. Para. 2.18 of the Code states:

If the nearest relative objects to an application being made for admission for treatment or reception into guardianship it cannot proceed at that time. If, because of the urgency of the case, and the risks of not taking forward the application immediately, it is thought necessary to proceed with the application, the ASW will then need to consider applying to the County Court for the nearest relative's 'displacement' (s29), and local authorities must provide proper assistance, especially legal assistance, in such cases. It is desirable for social services authorities to provide clear practical guidance on the procedures, and this should be discussed with the relevant County Courts.

ASWs should find out how quickly procedures can be followed locally. If it is not possible to take an application to County Court for displacement of the nearest relative within the time-scale of acceptable risk, those involved may need to consider if any other measures are needed (e.g. police involvement if an offence may occur or even the use of section 135(1)).

In the absence of test cases on these specific circumstances, some local authorities are reported to have received advice that a section 2 application might be appropriate but this is clearly contentious and advice should be sought locally. This problem would be resolved in any new legislation if all new detentions were for assessment (as per the Draft Bill) and could not be blocked by anyone. Such detention would be followed by an assessment as to whether longer-term intervention was needed. For now, professionals have to consider how best to respond if the problem occurs.

Short-term detentions and holding powers – sections 4, 135 and 5

These are second-best solutions compared with detention under sections 2 or 3. They are temporary responses to crises where circumstances do not allow a full assessment before invoking compulsory powers. Section 5 should not be used just to demonstrate to patients that they cannot leave hospital when they wish to. Each detention should be followed as soon as possible by an assessment of the need for further detention. The sections last for a maximum of 72 hours (this is timed from the moment when the patient is admitted to hospital or arrives at the place of safety) or until the assessment is completed, whichever is the sooner. They are not renewable, although section 4 can be converted to section 2 by the addition of a second medical recommendation and section 5(4) can change to 5(2) if a doctor deems this appropriate. None of the sections allows for an appeal to the MHRT (because of the short time period involved) and patients are not covered by consent to treatment procedures set out in Part IV of the Act. Therefore, these patients have the same right to refuse treatment as any informal patient.

Admission for assessment in cases of emergency – section 4

Where only one doctor is available and waiting for a second doctor would involve 'undesirable delay', it is possible to effect an admission under section 4. An application may be made by either an ASW or the nearest relative. Para. 6.2 of the Code states:

Section 4 should be used only in a genuine emergency, never for administrative convenience. 'Second doctors' should be available to assist with assessments prior to admission.

To meet the definition of emergency there must be evidence of: an immediate and significant risk of mental or physical harm to the patient or to others, and/or the danger of serious harm to property, and/or the need for physical restraint of the patient.

Apart from the urgent necessity for admission, grounds are basically the same as for section 2. The doctor providing the recommendation does not need to be section 12 approved and may not have previous acquaintance with the patient. This significantly reduces the safeguards for the patient and should be avoided if possible. It is important to remind the hospital to let the ASW know if the section is converted to section 2 so that the ASW can inform the nearest relative as required by section 11(3).

ASW reports for applications under sections 2, 3 or 4 (including advice on children)

Para. 11.13 of the Code states that the ASW should leave an outline report at the hospital when the patient is admitted, giving reasons for the admission and any practical matters about the patient's circumstances which the hospital should know and, where possible, the name and telephone number of a social worker who can give further information.

Local authority circular LAC(99)32 adds a suggested approach at para. 9.1:

(a) *In those instances where a compulsory admission is being considered, the needs of and arrangements for children involved with the patient should be considered by the ASW as an integral element within the assessment. This information should be recorded by the ASW and communicated to the hospital in the event of admission. The ASW should alert their colleagues in children's services if they have any concerns about child care arrangements for dependent children of the patient. It would assist this process if documents were designed to incorporate information from this element of the assessment.*

(b) *Similarly, the ASW should provide the hospital with information about the views of other person(s) with parental responsibility for the children of the patient, where it is appropriate to do so and if these can be ascertained. ASWs should be sensitive to situations where the relationship between parents has broken down so that any decision about child visiting is not used inappropriately in residence or contact disputes.*

(c) *In the vast majority of cases where no concerns are identified, arrangements should be made to support the patient and child and to facilitate contact.*

Warrant to search for and remove patients – section 135

This section covers two main sets of circumstances where an ASW, constable or other person might need to enter premises and remove a patient. Section.135 (1) states:

If it appears to a justice of the peace, on information on oath laid by an approved social worker, that there is reasonable cause to suspect that a person believed to be suffering from mental disorder:

(a) *has been, or is being, ill-treated, neglected or kept otherwise than under proper control, in any place within the jurisdiction of the justice, or*

(b) being unable to care for himself, is living alone in any such place,

the justice may issue a warrant authorising any constable … to enter, if need be by force, any premises specified in the warrant in which that person is believed to be, and, if thought fit, to remove him to a place of safety with a view to the making of an application in respect of him under Part II of this Act, or of other arrangements for his treatment or care.

In using the warrant, the constable needs to be accompanied by an ASW and by a doctor. As a result of a House of Lords decision in *Ward* v *Commissioner of Police*, magistrates may not apply additional requirements, e.g. naming the ASW, doctor or police officer who would have to then attend. Any ASW, doctor or police officer may attend.

The 'place of safety' to which the patient is taken could be a hospital, a police station, social services premises, or any suitable place where the occupier is willing to receive the patient. The patient may be kept there for up to 72 hours or until the assessment is completed, whichever is the sooner. Paragraph 315 of the Memorandum to the Act states that:

Only in exceptional circumstances, should a police station be used as a place of safety. If a police station is used, the patient should remain there for no longer than a few hours while an approved social worker makes the necessary arrangement for his removal elsewhere, either informally or under Part II of the Act.

Despite this advice there are many parts of the country where a police station is still the usual place of safety.

Section 135(2) covers circumstances where a patient liable to be taken to hospital or elsewhere under the Act appears to be on premises where entry has been refused or is likely to be refused. A constable (or other authorised person) may apply for a warrant which will authorise a constable to enter the premises and remove the patient. This might be used for a patient who has refused to return to hospital after a period of leave or who has absconded from hospital or from the place in which they are required to reside when subject to guardianship, or who is refusing to meet a requirement of supervised discharge.

Application in respect of patient already in hospital – section 5 (and implications of *HL* v *UK* [2004] – the 'Bournewood Gap')

Section 5 allows for detention of a person under sections 2 or 3 even if they are already an in-patient. It also contains provisions for preventing in-patients from leaving hospital where an assessment for detention under one of these sections is incomplete.

Under section 5(2) the doctor in charge of a patient's treatment (or, if absent, one nominee) may sign Form 12 stating that the patient should be detained under Part II of the Act. They pass the form to the hospital managers, who may detain the patient for up to 72 hours to enable a full assessment of the need for an application under sections 2 or 3 to take place. The patient could at this point be in any hospital, not necessarily a psychiatric unit. The power cannot be used to extend a section 2 or 3 which is about to expire.

For patients already receiving psychiatric treatment, there is provision under section 5(4) for specified nurses to detain them for up to six hours if they sign Form 13 indicating:

(a) that this patient, who is receiving treatment for mental disorder as an in-patient of this hospital is suffering from mental disorder to such a degree that it is necessary for the patient's health or safety or protection of others for that patient to be immediately restrained from leaving the hospital; and (b) it is not practicable to secure the immediate attendance of a registered medical practitioner for the purposes of furnishing a report under section 5(2) of the Mental Health Act 1983.

The 1993 version of the Code of Practice led to an interesting debate concerning the definition of an 'informal patient'. From the Percy Commission, which led to the 1959 Act, there was a presumption that a 'non-objecting' patient should be grouped with those consenting rather than those dissenting. This meant that professionals involved in the admission procedure tended not to use compulsion where there was an absence of dissent. The definition of an informal patient, however, given in the 1993 Code for the purposes of section 5, suggested that there should have been active consent:

> 8.4 An informal in-patient, for the purposes of this Section, is one who has understood and accepted the offer of a bed, who has freely appeared on the ward and who has co-operated in the admission procedure. The Section, for example, cannot be used for an out-patient attending a hospital's accident and emergency department.

The last sentence may give an indication of the area this advice was supposed to clarify. Some lawyers have argued that 'non-objecting', compliant but effectively detained patients (*de facto* detained patients) should not be treated in hospital unless they are formally detained under the provisions of the Act.

This issue was addressed in the *L* v *Bournewood Community and Mental Health NHS Trust* case. In December 1997, the Appeal Court ruled that where a hospital had the intention and the ability to prevent a patient from leaving, then the patient was, in effect, detained and should therefore be so detained by the Mental Health Act if they were to be kept in hospital and treated. This ruling gave such patients the protection offered by the Act (e.g. consent to treatment rules and the role of Mental Health Act Commission). In June 1998, however, the House of Lords ruled that a compliant mentally incapacitated patient could effectively be detained and treated in hospital. If the patient subsequently showed signs of being unwilling to remain in hospital, they should be assessed with a view to possible detention (see Health Service Circular (HSC1998/9990)).

The revised form of words in the third edition of the Code of Practice is as follows:

> 8.4 For the purposes of s.5(2), informal patients are usually voluntary patients, that is, those who have the capacity to consent and who consent to enter hospital for in-patient treatment. Patients who lack the capacity to consent but do not object to admission for treatment may also be informal patients (see para. 2.8). The section cannot be used for an out-patient attending a hospital's accident and emergency department. Admission procedures should not be implemented with the sole intention of then using the power in section 5(2).

Para. 2.8 referred to here states:

> If at the time of admission, the patient is mentally incapable of consent, but does not object to entering hospital and receiving care or treatment, admission should be

informal ... The decision to admit a mentally incapacitated patient informally should be made by the doctor in charge of the patient's treatment in accordance with what is in the patient's best interest and is justifiable on the basis of the common law doctrine of necessity ... If a patient lacks capacity at the time of an assessment or review, it is particularly important that both clinical and social care requirements are considered, and that account is taken of the patient's ascertainable wishes and feelings and the views of their immediate relatives and carers on what would be in the patient's best interests.

HL v *The United Kingdom*, European Court Judgment, October 2004

This final court stage of the Bournewood saga has profound implications for English mental health law. Extracts from the judgment are reproduced below. The Department of Health's initial response can be found at Appendix 2 to this guide.

The applicant was born in 1949 and lives in Surrey. He has suffered from autism since birth. He is unable to speak and his level of understanding is limited. He is frequently agitated and has a history of self-harming behaviour. He lacks the capacity to consent or object to medical treatment. For over 30 years he was cared for in Bournewood Hospital ... He was an in-patient at the Intensive Behavioural Unit (IBU) from 1987. The applicant's responsible medical officer (who had cared for him since 1977) was Dr M ... In March 1994 he was discharged on a trial basis to paid carers, Mr and Mrs E, with whom he successfully resided until 22 July 1997 [when] he was at the day centre when he became particularly agitated, hitting himself on the head with his fists and banging his head against the wall. Staff could not contact Mr and Mrs E and got in touch with a local doctor who administered a sedative.

HL remained agitated and on the recommendation of the local authority care services manager (AF) with overall responsibility for the applicant, he was taken to the A & E unit at the hospital. He was seen by a psychiatrist (Dr P) and transferred to the IBU. It is recorded that he made no attempt to leave. 'Dr P and Dr M considered that the best interests of the applicant required his admission for in-patient treatment'. Dr M considered detention under the 1983 Act but concluded it 'was not necessary as the applicant was compliant and did not resist admission'. Dr M later confirmed that she would have recommended HL's detention if he had resisted admission. The carers were discouraged from visiting at this point. In a report on 18 August Dr M concluded that HL suffered from a mood disorder as well as autism and that his discharge would be against medical opinion.

On 29 October 1997 the Court of Appeal indicated it would decide the appeal in the applicant's favour. HL was then held on section 5(2) and on 31 October an application for section 3 was made. On 2 November he was seen by his carers for the first time since July.

Application was made to the MHRT in November and independent psychiatric reports were obtained recommending HL's discharge. Before the MHRT hearing application was also made for a Managers' Hearing. On 5 December HL was allowed home on section 17 leave and on 12 December the Managers discharged him from the section 3.

Procedural safeguards for those detained under the Mental Health Act 1983

The European Court noted the following safeguards:

(a) statutory criteria need to be met and applied by two doctors and an applicant

(b) Part IV consent to treatment procedures

(c) applications and automatic referrals to MH Review Tribunals

(d) nearest-relative powers (including discharge powers)

(e) section 117 after-care

(f) the Code of Practice and the Mental Health Act Commission

(g) section 132 rights to information.

Decision of the European Court

The key is Article 5, Right to liberty and security of person:

No one shall be deprived of their liberty except for specific cases and in accordance with procedure prescribed by law, e.g. after conviction, lawful arrest on suspicion of having committed an offence, lawful detention of person of unsound mind, to prevent spread of infectious diseases. Everyone deprived of liberty by arrest or detention shall be entitled to take proceedings by which the lawfulness of the detention shall be decided speedily by a Court and release ordered if the detention is not lawful.

The Court concluded that HL was 'deprived of his liberty' within the meaning of Article 5.1 of the European Convention on Human Rights. It was not crucial that the door was locked or lockable. 'The Court considers the key factor in the present case to be that the health care professionals treating and managing the applicant exercised complete and effective control over his care and movements from the moment he presented acute behavioural problems on 22 July 1997 to the date he was compulsorily detained on 29 October 1997.' It was clear that 'the applicant would only be released from the hospital to the care of Mr and Mrs E as and when those professionals considered it appropriate'. HL 'was under continuous supervision and control and was not free to leave'.

The Court accepted that HL was suffering from a mental disorder of a kind or degree warranting compulsory confinement. However, the Court found that there had been a breach of Article 5.1 in that there was an absence of procedural safeguards to protect against arbitrary deprivation of liberty in the reliance on the common law doctrine of necessity. Article 5.4 was also breached in that the applicant had no right to have the lawfulness of his detention reviewed speedily by a court. Judicial review and habeas corpus proceedings were not adequate. The Court did not find there had been a breach of Article 14.

Implications

Each case will need to be looked at on its own merits but in a situation similar to that of HL it is unlikely to be safe to rely on the common law, especially where the criteria for detention under the Mental Health Act appear to be met.

The Department of Health initial guidance was published in December 2004 and is reprinted in Appendix 2. Key paragraphs state:

32. Until these safeguards are established in law, the effect of the judgment is that it would be unlawful for an NHS body or a local authority (without the prior authorisation of the High Court) to arrange or provide care or treatment for an incapacitated patient in a way that amounted to deprivation of liberty within the meaning of article 5 of the Convention, unless the patient were detained under the Mental Health Act 1983. *33. Nonetheless, the NHS and local authorities will need to continue to provide care and treatment for incapacitated patients, and it is important that neither the safety of those patients nor the quality of the care they receive is jeopardised during the interim period.* *34. Pending the development of new safeguards described above, NHS bodies and local authorities will want to consider what steps they can take in the short term to protect incapacitated people against the risk of arbitrary deprivation of liberty and minimise the risk of further successful legal challenges.*

The Department of Health has issued a consultation document on the 'Bournewood Gap'. It is not clear at the time of writing to whether the Mental Capacity Act will be amended or if the issue will be addressed in any forthcoming Mental Health Bill.

Two-stage approach to a Mental Health Act assessment

The first important step in any intervention is to assess a person's mental health. If they have a mental disorder of a nature or degree which warrants compulsory intervention one can then move to the chart below.

Check the chart to note significance of different risk criteria for detention and guardianship. (The chart is on an imagined scale from no risk at the bottom to extremely high at the top.)

100%	(e.g. certain death if person not detained)
	In any case where a person was seen by the RMO to be above this line, the RMO would bar any attempt by the nearest relative to discharge the patient
very high	Patient if discharged would be likely to act in a manner dangerous to others or self
	In any case where a person was seen to be above this line they could be detained under section 3 (s2 grounds are similar) but could be discharged by the nearest relative giving 72 hours' notice unless RMO blocks as above
high	Detention necessary for health or safety of patient or for the protection of other persons
	In any case where a person was seen to be above this line they could be received into guardianship under s7 but could be discharged by nearest relative at any time
less	Guardianship necessary in interest of welfare of patient or the protection of others
	On this scale, there can be no compulsory intervention until at least the grounds for guardianship are met.
0%	No perceived risk

There is particular significance where a person is seen to be within the area between 'high' and 'very high' risk levels. The nearest relative would be able to order the patient's discharge (giving 72 hours' notice) but the RMO would be unable to block this as they do not perceive the patient as dangerous. If the RMO and the ASW nevertheless consider that the patient should still be detained (i.e. the nearest relative's intervention has not altered the situation to drop the risk level below the middle line marked 'high'), the ASW should consider making an application to the County Court for the displacement of the nearest relative under section 29.

Guardianship under the Mental Health Act 1983

Introduction

The Code of Practice (Para. 13.1) states:

> *The purpose of guardianship is to enable patients to receive care in the community where it cannot be provided without the use of compulsory powers. It provides an authoritative framework for working with a patient, with a minimum of constraint, to achieve as independent a life as possible within the community.*

Numbers

Guardianship is used in a limited way and in comparatively small numbers in England and Wales. It will be interesting to see if its use for mentally incapacitated patients increases at all as a result of the *HL* v *UK* (Bournewood) judgment. The Department of Health's consultation on the 'Bournewood Gap' includes a consideration of community-based patients and not just those in hospital.

The use of guardianship varies considerably in different areas. Overall its use has settled down since 2000 after significant increases in the 1990s. From a very low base of 60 new guardianships in England in 1983–4, the numbers increased to 139 new cases in 1988–9 and 672 in 1999–2000. The number of new cases then declined to 466 new cases in 2004–05.

It is also possible to look at guardianship in terms of continuing cases on a given date. Here the numbers stabilised earlier as people tend to stay in guardianship for longer periods than in the 1980s. On 31 March 2005, there were 966 people in guardianship compared with 161 in 1984. The graph in Figure 2.1 illustrates the changes in use of guardianship and the table below shows the significant variations around the country.

Supervised after-care was introduced in 1996. It provides similar powers to guardianship but is only available to patients who have been detained on long-term sections. The publicity around its introduction may have contributed to increased use of guardianship in the late 1990s.

Applications for guardianship

Guardianship may be applied for through a civil route (s7) or, very infrequently, via the courts (s37). For civil admissions, the applicant may be an approved social worker or the nearest relative as defined in section 26. The application is based on two medical recommendations and is made to the local authority. Social services departments vary in their procedures for making decisions on guardianship applications and some are negative in their attitude to this piece of legislation. The relevant local authority is the one where the patient lives unless the guardian is a private individual, when their address determines the relevant authority. Guardianship lasts up to six months, is renewable for a further six months and then yearly.

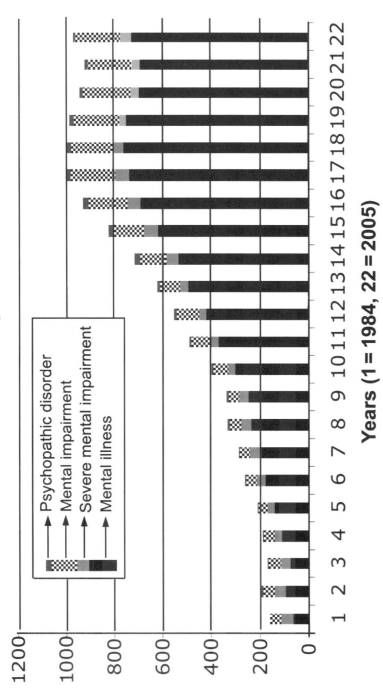

Figure 2.1. Guardianships 1984–2005

The guardian may be the local authority or a private individual approved by the local authority. However, private individuals hardly ever act as guardians. For example, in 2004 there were 925 cases where the local authority was the guardian and only seven where the guardian was a private individual.

The guardian's powers are set out in section 8(1) and give the guardian:

(a) the power to require the patient to reside at a place specified by the authority or person named as guardian;

(b) the power to require the patient to attend at places and times so specified for the purpose of medical treatment, occupation, education or training;

(c) the power to require access to the patient to be given, at any place where the patient is residing, to any medical practitioner, approved social worker or other person so specified.

Para. 40 of the Memorandum to the 1983 Act suggests that guardianship:

(a) may be used to discourage the patient from sleeping rough or living with people who may exploit or mistreat him, or to ensure that he resides in a particular hostel or other facility

(b) could include a local authority day centre, or a hospital, surgery or clinic

(c) could be used, for example, to ensure that the patient did not neglect himself.

The powers are essentially the same as those for Supervised Aftercare but, unlike the more recent provision, there is no power within guardianship to convey except where the person has absconded from the place of residence. Note that Part IV of the Act on consent to treatment does not apply to guardianship. Thus there is no statutory route to make a patient accept treatment, such as medication, against their will. Because guardianship does not give any powers in relation to property and affairs it sometimes goes hand in hand with use of the Court of Protection.

The 1959 Mental Health Act gave greater powers to the guardian (as if they were the parent of a child under 14) and it was considered that this may have been one cause of its limited use. There is one other major change compared with the earlier Act, and this has led to serious problems. The change from 'subnormality' to 'mental impairment' drastically reduced the use of guardianship with people with learning disabilities. Many people who might benefit are excluded from guardianship as a result of the definition of 'mental impairment', i.e. requiring abnormal aggression or seriously irresponsible conduct. In contrast, the inclusion of dementia within the classification of 'mental illness' has led to a significant increase in the use of guardianship with this group.

There is a myth that guardianship cannot be used to place people in residential care. The Code of Practice (at Para. 13.10) states:

> *where an adult is assessed as requiring residential care but owing to mental incapacity is unable to make a decision as to whether he or she wishes to be placed in residential care, those who are responsible for his or her care should consider the applicability and appropriateness of guardianship.*

The revisions to the Code, introduced in 1999, also contained new advice on the degree of co-operation needed, i.e. 'depending on the patient's level of "capacity", his or her recognition of the authority of and willingness to work with the guardian' are needed. 'The guardian should be willing to advocate on behalf of the patient in relation to those agencies whose services are needed to carry out the care plan.'

The grounds for using guardianship

No one under the age of 16 can be received into guardianship. For a mentally disordered child under 16 who requires some supervision in the community, child care law (including the rights of parents and the local authority) is available.

The grounds for guardianship under section 7 or section 37 are similar. Section 7(2) states:

A guardianship application may be made in respect of a patient on the grounds that:

(a) *he is suffering from mental disorder, being mental illness, severe mental impairment, psychopathic disorder or mental impairment and his mental disorder is of a nature or degree which warrants his reception into guardianship under this section; and*

(b) *it is necessary in the interests of the welfare of the patient or for the protection of other persons that the patient should be so received.*

Note that the mental disorder must be one of the four specific classifications, as with a detention for treatment under section 3, that is: mental illness; severe mental impairment; mental impairment; or psychopathic disorder. This means that 'arrested or incomplete development of mind' is not sufficient and must be associated with abnormally aggressive or seriously irresponsible conduct, thus becoming mental impairment.

Continuing guardianships at 31.03.05 for some local authorities and total for England

Local authority	Total	Population	Per 100,000
Halton (Widnes)	12	118,208	10.15
Middlesbrough	13	143,000	9.09
Liverpool	34	450,000	7.56
Bolton	15	260,000	5.77
Southampton	11	215,000	5.12
Isle of Wight	6	135,000	4.44
Bath	6	170,000	3.53
West Berkshire	5	145,000	3.45
Hertfordshire	32	1,004,600	3.19
Gloucestershire	15	528,370	2.84
Bournemouth	4	163,400	2.45
Bristol	9	380,615	2.36
Bexley	5	217,200	2.30
Hampshire	25	1,248,800	2.00
Cornwall	10	506,100	1.98
Plymouth	5	255,000	1.96
Devon	12	629,400	1.91
Wiltshire	8	433,500	1.85
Swindon	3	180,000	1.67
Manchester	7	439,540	1.59

Local authority	Total	Population	Per 100,000
Portsmouth	3	190,400	1.58
Greenwich	3	215,500	1.39
Kensington & Chelsea	2	159,000	1.26
Lewisham	3	247,000	1.21
Somerset	6	498,093	1.20
Merton	2	184,315	1.09
North Somerset	2	190,000	1.05
Dorset	4	389,223	1.03
Westminster	2	194,289	1.03
Barnet	3	314,000	0.96
South Gloucestershire	2	239,000	0.84
Lambeth	2	261,150	0.77
Poole	1	141,000	0.71
Southwark	2	283,000	0.71
Bromley	2	295,330	0.68
Hounslow	1	209,513	0.48
Surrey	5	1,100,000	0.45
Croydon	1	340,000	0.29
Sutton	0	178,000	0.00
Hillingdon	0	231,602	0.00
Torbay	0	122,900	0.00
Wandsworth	0	69,290	0.00
Ealing	0	311,000	0.00
Richmond upon Thames	0	183,774	0.00
Brent	0	249,511	0.00
Kingston	0	150,161	0.00
Totals	283	14,769,784	1.92
Total England	966	49,855,000	1.94

Sources: NHS and Social Services Directory 2004-05 (*Guardian*), Government Statistical Services.

Supervised after-care

Introduction

This measure is also sometimes referred to as Supervised Discharge. It was one of three amendments to the Act which were introduced in 1996. Changes concerning leave of absence and patients absent without leave are dealt with elsewhere. Public reaction to apparent examples of a breakdown in community care arrangements (e.g. Christopher Clunis in 1992 and Ben Silcock in 1993) plus concern with 'revolving-door' patients were factors which contributed to the introduction of supervised aftercare. The Government believed that a small group of patients needed closer supervision than was being provided at the time. It was linked to the Care Programme Approach based on section 117 after-care which are described later in this chapter.

There were 187 new supervised after-care cases in England when it was first used in 1996–7, 562 new cases three years later in 1999–2000, and figures levelled at 608 new cases in 2003–04. Most trusts have only a few new cases each year (e.g. Portsmouth had five in 2003–04) but a few used it more often (e.g. in the same year South London and Maudsley had 25 new cases; Devon partnership 27; South West London and St Georges 21; Hampshire Partnership 14).

Supervised after-care was seen primarily as a health measure. It looks like guardianship (with additional powers to convey, and driven by health rather than social services) but the government saw it as separate and targeting a different group of patients. It is interesting to note, despite the emphasis on it being a health-led measure with CPNs seen as the most likely supervisors, in Scotland the role was taken on by a social worker, the Mental Health Officer (equivalent to ASW). Comparisons between the two systems are interesting. Note that the Scottish system has also recently been amended.

What is the purpose?

- to ensure that the patient receives s117 after-care services when they leave hospital

- to provide formal supervision after discharge.

To whom does it apply?

Patient must be 16 and liable to be detained under one of the following sections:

3 admission for treatment

37 hospital order (made by Magistrates' or Crown Court)

47 transfer direction of sentenced prisoner (by Home Secretary, without restrictions)

48 transfer direction of prisoners who have not been sentenced (made by the Home Secretary, without restrictions).

> *Notes:* (i) patients could be on s17 leave when s25A is applied for and accepted
> (ii) patients could agree to stay on in hospital, informally, for a period before leaving, and the application would then take effect when they leave hospital.

What are the grounds?

- patient suffering from specific mental disorder (as for s3)

- there would be a substantial risk of serious harm to the health or safety of the patient, or the safety of other persons, or of the patient being seriously exploited, if they were not to receive section 117 after-care

- being subject to after-care under supervision is likely to help secure that the patient receives such services.

'Substantial risk' means more than remote and not merely minimal [*Att-Gen* v *English* (1982)]. The second part of each of these tests refers to the potential negative outcome.

Who is involved in the process?

(Further details under 'Procedure' below)

- the responsible medical officer makes the application on Form 1S

- the application is addressed to the relevant health authority

- the health authority must consult with the relevant social services department to formulate the section 117 after-care plan on which this is based

- recommendations are needed from a doctor (Form 2S) and an ASW (Form 3S)

- signatures of proposed CRMO and Supervisor to indicate they will take on role.

Jones (2004) is of the opinion that, as long as the application is signed while the patient is still liable to be detained, the patient's detention might lapse before the section 25A is accepted.

What is the effect?

There will be a:

- community responsible medical officer (CRMO)

- supervisor (e.g. CPN, SW, or other – usually the Care Co-ordinator)

- record of planned after-care services and any requirements placed on the individual.

How long does it last?

- six months, renewable for six months, and then annually

- the patient and NR can appeal to the Mental Health Review Tribunal once in each period

What powers are conferred?

Under section 25D after-care bodies may impose any of the following requirements, that:

(a) the patient reside at a specified place

(b) the patient attend at specified places and times for the purpose of medical treatment, occupation, education or training

(c) access to the patient be given, at any place where the patient is residing, to the supervisor, any registered medical practitioner or any ASW or to any other person authorised by the supervisor.

> *Notes:* (i) Power to take and convey exists for (a) and (b) when they are made requirements.
> (ii) A patient is not covered by Part IV of the Act so consent to treatment provisions do not apply and the patient cannot be made to take medication unwillingly.

However, various research papers published in the psychiatric Bulletin since 2000 (e.g. Franklin *et al.*) suggest that supervised after-care improves compliance with prescribed medication.

What must the patient be told if subject to supervised after-care?

Where the health authority accepts a supervision application they must inform the patient, both orally and in writing:

- that the application has been accepted

- of its effects on the patient

- of their right to appeal to the Mental Health Review Tribunal.

Can the after-care requirements be modified?

Yes. Before or after discharge from hospital, the responsible after-care bodies can review and, if appropriate, modify the services or the requirements. The patient, carer and nearest relative (where appropriate) must be consulted. If the review is because the patient refuses or neglects to receive any of the after-care services provided or to comply with any of the specified requirements, then there must be a review of whether supervised after-care is still needed and whether admission for treatment might be necessary. In the latter case, an ASW must be informed. Any compulsory admission then requires new medical recommendations and an application.

How should requirements be worded?

They need to be specific enough for the patient to understand and comply with them but not so specific that they would regularly need changing (one problem here is that changes have to be formalised and recorded on the pink forms). The patient might, for example, be required to attend a specified facility on days to be notified by the supervisor.

How does supervised after-care end?

- The CRMO can end supervised after-care at any time, but must consult with the patient, the supervisor and certain other persons before doing so (section 25H).

- It ends automatically if a patient is detained on s3 or is accepted into guardianship.

- The MHRT can discharge the patient from supervised after-care on application from the patient or the nearest relative or referral from the Secretary of State.

What if a patient on supervised after-care is detained on s2 or is in custody?

Supervised after-care is suspended and resumes when the patient is back in the community.

When supervised after-care ends, does section 117 after-care also end?

No. Not necessarily. Health and social services authorities have to agree that a person no longer needs such services before the obligation to provide them ends.

Supervised after-care: the power to convey (s25D of Mental Health Act 1983)

A Supervisor only has power to convey a patient to a place where they are required to reside or attend where these requirements are specified on the application.

Guidance on supervised after-care [HSG(96)11/LAC(96)8]

- Advises inter-agency protocol to cover when power to convey may be used.

- Supervisor may decide to use the power if a patient has got into a situation which is putting him or her, or other people, at risk and needs to be taken home urgently.

- The supervisor may also wish to consider using the power if the patient is not attending for medical treatment and it is thought that this might be overcome by taking him or her to the place where the treatment is to be given.

- Supervisor should consider whether problems could be overcome by adjustment to package of services or if an assessment for readmission might be necessary.

- The supervisor may authorise any responsible adult to convey. It will normally be advisable to use the ambulance service and possibly the police.

- Reasons for use of the power must always be recorded.

Supervised after-care or guardianship? HSG/LAC guidance

Paragraph 8 notes that guardianship remains available as an option but considers that for patients who meet requirements for supervised discharge the latter has advantages in the specific legal provision it offers for making and reviewing after-care arrangements and the roles assigned to the community responsible medical officer and supervisor.

Where the grounds for supervised discharge are not fully met, the guidance states that guardianship may well be considered.

A comparison of supervised after-care (s25A) with guardianship (s7)

(from *Mental Health Law: A Practical Guide* (Puri *et al.*, 2005)

	After-care under supervision	Guardianship
Existing status	Aged at least 16 and liable to detention on ss3, 37, 47 or 48	Aged at least 16
Mental disorder	Mental illness Severe mental impairment Mental impairment Psychopathic disorder	Mental illness Severe mental impairment Mental impairment Psychopathic disorder
Risk level	There would be a substantial risk of serious harm to health or safety of patient, safety of others, or of serious exploitation of patient if not to receive s117 after-care	Necessary in the interests of the welfare of the patient or for the protection of others
Application by	RMO	ASW or nearest relative
Recommendations	ASW + doctor	2 doctors
Who accepts?	Health Authority	Local Authority
Duration	6 months, 6 months, yearly	6 months, 6 months, yearly
Mental Health Review Tribunal	Patient or Nearest Relative (where informed) can apply	Patient can apply
Who can discharge?	CRMO and MHRT	RMO, MHRT, Nearest Relative, Local Authority
When does it end automatically?	If detained on section 3 or placed in guardianship	If detained on section 3
Requirements	Reside where specified Attend for treatment etc. Access as authorised	Reside where specified Attend for treatment etc. Access as authorised
Power to convey?	Yes, where requirement made for residence and/or attendance	No, but power to return to required place of residence
Part IV Consent to Treatment rules?	Not covered by Part IV	Not covered by Part IV
Will s117 after-care apply?	Yes	Only if patient previously on s3, 37, 47 or 48
Covered by CPA	Yes	Yes

Procedure for obtaining supervised after-care

The RMO considers application and ensures that the following are consulted:

- the patient

- one or more members of the hospital-based team

- one or more professionals concerned with the after-care services

- informal carer (not professional) WHO RMO thinks will play substantial part in care

- nearest relative (unless patient objects and not overruled) if practicable.

By involving social services in the above process this should link with the health authority's requirement to consult with the SSD about a section 117 plan. A statement of after-care services to be provided is needed and should be attached to the application.

The application is normally submitted to the health provider unit and must include the names of the CRMO and supervisor as well as the nearest relative and informal carer if consulted. Application to be accompanied by:

- Two recommendations from the ASW and doctor. (They should try to see the patient together or at least within a week of each other. They should also examine records of detention and treatment and the plans for after-care.)

- Signed statements from the CRMO and supervisor that they are willing to act as such.

- Statement of after-care services (in a care plan).

- Details of requirements to be imposed on patient.

Joint protocols on supervised after-care

HSG/LAC Guidance recommends HAs and LAs should develop local protocols. (Para. 9). Annex C suggests such inter-agency agreements should cover the following:

Shared understanding needed on:

- risk assessment procedure

- consultation procedures between HA/provider unit and LA for consideration of section 25A, completion of documentation, acceptance of application

- reviewing and monitoring

- role of supervisor and experience required

- power to convey: when to use or not use, records, who is authorised, involving ambulance and police

- appeals and complaints.

Making the procedure work:

- how to provide advocacy and interpretation

- what joint procedures to use if the patient does not attend for treatment

- integration of CPA, Care Management and section 25A

- IT systems to integrate CPA with supervision registers

- performance standards

- involvement of users and carers.

Implementation planning:

- training for supervisors and other professionals

- after-care arrangements discussed with probation, housing police and GPs.

Leave of absence and absence without leave

Section 17 leave under the Mental Health Act 1983

This provision was amended in 1996 at the same time as supervised after-care was introduced. The amendment effectively increased the length of time for which a patient can be on leave. The main features of section 17 leave are as follows:

- The RMO may grant leave to any patient liable to be detained under Part II of the Act to enable them to be absent from the hospital.

- Hospital order (s 37; see Chapter 5) patients may be granted leave by the RMO but restricted patients may be granted leave only with the Home Secretary's permission.

- It is probably the case that patients subject to s35, 36 or 38 may not be granted leave without consent of the court on the basis that they are still subject to court jurisdiction.

- Leave may be subject to any conditions the RMO thinks necessary in the interests of the patient or for the protection of others. It may be granted indefinitely, on specified occasions, or for a specific period. It may not go beyond the renewal date for the section.

- A patient could be granted leave to another hospital (e.g. nearer home or where physical treatment is needed) and could later be transferred under section 19.

- The RMO may direct the patient should remain in custody when on leave.

- The RMO may revoke leave in writing and recall the patient to hospital if they consider it necessary in the interest of the patient's health or safety or for the protection of others.

- A patient may not be recalled to hospital for the sole purpose of renewing the detention.

- A patient on leave is still liable to be detained and therefore is still subject to the consent to treatment provisions of Part IV of the Act.

- The duty to provide section 117 after-care applies when a patient is on leave (CoP para. 27.3).

- An application for supervised aftercare could be made while a patient is on leave.

The revised Code also includes two important statements:

> 20.3a *Unrestricted patients. The RMO cannot delegate the decision to grant leave of absence to any other doctor or professional. The RMO is responsible for undertaking any appropriate consultation, and may make leave subject to*

> *conditions which he or she considers necessary in the interests of the patient or for the protection of other people. Only the RMO can grant leave of absence to a patient formally detained under the Act. In the absence of the RMO (e.g. if he/she is on annual leave or otherwise unavailable), permission can only be granted by the doctor who is for the time being in charge of the patient's treatment. Where practicable, this should be another consultant psychiatrist, locum consultant or specialist registrar approved under section 12(2) of the Act. The granting of leave cannot be vetoed by the hospital managers.*

> 20.4   *The RMO may decide to authorise short-term local leave, which may be managed by other staff. For example, the patient may be given leave for a shopping trip of two hours every week, with the decision on the particular two hours left to the discretion of the responsible nursing staff. It is crucial that such decisions fall within the terms of the grant of periodic leave by the RMO, and that he or she reviews decisions and their implementation from time to time and explicitly records the outcome in writing.*

A patient liable to be detained under s3 may have this renewed, even if on leave, if the RMO considers that there is a hospital element to the treatment plan (*B* v *Barking, Havering and Brentwood Community Healthcare NHS Trust,* 1999, 1FLR 106, together with *R. (on the application of D.R.)* v *Mersey Care NHS Trust*, 2002 and *R (CS)* v *MHRT,* 2004). This last case involved a patient who had been on section 17 leave for three months. Hospital attendance was limited to a four-weekly ward round, and weekly sessions with ward psychologist. The judge noted that it was:

> *clear to me the RMO was engaged in a delicate balancing exercise by which she was, with as light a touch as she could, encouraging progress to discharge. Her purpose was to break the persistent historical cycle of admission, serious relapse and readmission. It may be that in the closing stages of the treatment in hospital her grasp on the claimant was gossamer thin, but to view that grasp as insignificant is, in my view, to misunderstand the evidence.*

With a broad definition of what amounts to a hospital. Section 17 leave in some cases is virtually a community treatment order.

Absence without leave (s 18)

When a detained patient is absent without leave he or she may be taken into custody and returned to hospital. Changes in 1996 extended the period during which patients on long-term sections may be so taken. This is six months or the end of the period of detention, whichever is longer. If the detention section has lapsed, the patient may be detained for a week for the RMO to examine the patient and consider a possible renewal of detention.

For any patient who is returned having been absent without leave for more than 28 days, the RMO must consult an ASW and one or more other professionals who have been concerned with the patient's medical treatment.

If the power of entry is needed but refused, consideration should be given to the use of section 135(2) or the police powers under section 17(1)(d) of the Police and Criminal Evidence Act 1984. When a patient in guardianship absents themselves without permission from any place where they are required to reside, they may be taken into custody and returned to that place.

Discharge and after-care of patients under section 117

The purpose of after-care is stated in Para. 27.1 of the Code of Practice as follows:

While the Act defines after-care requirements only in very broad terms, it is clear that a central purpose of all treatment and care is to equip patients to cope with life outside hospital and function there successfully without danger to themselves or other people. The planning of this needs to start when the patient is admitted to hospital.

General issues concerning after-care are considered in the following part of this chapter which covers the Care Programme Approach.

Section 117 places a specific duty on health and social services authorities (in co-operation with relevant voluntary agencies) to provide after-care to a patient who has been detained under sections 3, 37, 45A, 47 or 48 and is discharged and leaves hospital.

- The requirement still applies even if there is a gap between the date when the section is lifted and the date when the patient leaves hospital.

- There is a need to assess needs of each individual to whom this section applies.

- The services should continue to be provided until both the health and social services authorities are satisfied that the person concerned no longer needs the services.

- Supervised after-care introduced the possibility of requiring the patient to accept the services (see Chapter 2).

- Services provided under section 117 are community care services for the purposes of the NHS and Community Care Act 1990.

- If a need is then identified it must be provided but there is probably discretion as to the level and precise nature of the service. (*R* v *Gloucestershire CC ex p. Barry* (1997))

Proper implementation of the CPA should ensure that the legal requirements of section 117 are met. Authorities should be able to identify clearly which patients are covered by section 117.

Charging for services

This has been a contentious area for some years. Essentially section 117 services should be free. The Bournewood case also drew attention to the fact that there are some benefits of being detained on section 3 in that residential and domiciliary services can be very expensive and may become free for someone who has been detained.

In *R. v Manchester City Council, ex p. Stennet*t (2002) the House of Lords ruled that section 117 imposes a freestanding duty to provide after-care services rather than being a passport to services provided under other legislation. There is no power to charge people for section 117 services and therefore they must be provided free. This would include any medication which was part of the patients psychiatric treatment. A number of authorities have had to reimburse people as a result of the Stennett judgement.

General services

See National Assistance Act 1948 and NHS Act 1977. Note that DoH Circular LAC(93)10 sets out arrangements for provision of social services which apply to mentally disordered persons:

accommodation; social work service; social rehabilitation; occupational, social and recreational facilities. These are considered in more detail in Chapter 9.

Section 133 requires hospital managers to give the nearest relative notice of intention to discharge a detained patient (except if patient or nearest relative has requested otherwise). If practicable, this notice should be given at least seven days before the intended date of discharge. This provision applies to all discharges from detention, and not just to section 3. Carers have suggested that this provision is frequently ignored by hospitals (see Chapter 3). Hospital managers must take reasonable steps to identify the patient's nearest relative.

Care Programme Approach and National Service Framework

The Care Programme Approach (CPA) was introduced in England by circular HC(90)23, LASSL(90)11. It came into effect in 1991. It was an attempt to provide some structure to the complicated range of services that existed to meet the needs of mentally ill people outside hospital. CPA requires health authorities, in collaboration with local authorities, to make arrangements for the care and treatment of mentally ill people in the community. It was introduced in Wales in 2004. The four main elements of CPA as set out in the MH Act Code of Practice at Para. 1.2 are:

- systematic arrangements for assessing people's health and social care needs

- the formulation of a care plan which addresses those needs

- the appointment of a key worker to keep in close touch with the patient and monitor care

- regular review, and if need be, agreed changes to the care plan.

This was revised in the light of the Mental Health National Service Framework and the lessons learned since 1991. The current arrangements are set out in a policy booklet *Effective Care and Co-Ordination in Mental Health Services* published in 1999. This made CPA less bureaucratic and better integrated with care management. The CPA applies to all adults of working age in contact with the secondary mental health system (health and social care). The principles also apply to people of other ages and transitions between services should be carefully managed.

Summary of key points from the 1999 policy document

Achieving Integration
21. *CPA will be integrated with Care Management in all areas to form a single care co-ordination approach for adults of working age with mental health problems.*
22. *Each health and social services mental health provider must jointly identify a Lead Officer with Authority to work across all agencies to deliver an integrated approach to the CPA and Care Management.*
23. *The CPA is not simply an 'after-care arrangement'. As a framework for mental health care, the CPA is as applicable to service users in residential settings (including prisons) as to those in the community. Assertive inreach is as relevant as assertive outreach as an underpinning principle of the CPA.*

Achieving Consistency
24. *Two levels of the CPA must be introduced: (i) Standard, (ii) Enhanced.*
25. *The requirement to maintain a supervision register will be removed.*
26. *The Key Worker will be known as the Care Co-ordinator.*

Achieving a More Streamlined Approach

27. Implementation of CPA should not place undue burden on professionals whose prime responsibility is to care for service users; it should facilitate that care.

28. Review and evaluation of care planning should be regarded as ongoing processes and the requirement for a nationally determined review period, i.e. six-monthly, will be removed. At each review meeting, however, the date of the next review must be set and recorded. Any member of the care team or the user or carer must also be able to ask for a review at any time. Annual audit should ensure that reviews are carried out.

29. Local service providers should ensure that a system is in place to collect data on all service users, including total numbers in contact with services and the numbers whose care is managed through enhanced and standard CPA.

30. Local audit should move away from a focus on simple numbers and more towards assessing the quality of CPA implementation, including the quality of care plans, the attainment of treatment goals and, particularly for those with multiple needs, the effectiveness of inter-agency working. The views of service users are an effective indicator of the quality of services and must be included in any audit of service delivery.

Achieving a Proper Focus

31. Risk assessment is an essential and ongoing part of the CPA process. Care plans for severely mentally ill service users should include urgent follow-up within one week of hospital discharge. Care plans for all those requiring enhanced CPA should include a 'what to do in a crisis' and a contingency plan.

32. Those who use mental health services deserve a framework for care co-ordination which recognises and responds to diversity. The care plan must reflect this diversity through proper attention to the service user's culture, ethnicity, gender and sexuality.

33. The process of the CPA is clearly intended to deliver care to meet the individual needs of service users. Those needs often relate not just to their own lives, but also to the lives of their wider family. The CPA should take account of this, in particular of the needs of children and of carers of people with mental health problems, and must comply with the Carers (Recognition and Services) Act 1995 and the National Service Framework standard on caring for carers.

Responsibility for Implementation

34. The responsibility for implementation of the changes summarised above rests with the Chief Executive of the Mental Health provider Trust in conjunction with their partner Directors of Social Services. Changes to the CPA need to be built into the overall strategic response to mental health services development, in line with the National Service Framework. Changes in the CPA should have the full support and involvement of all the partners in the mental health system, including primary care and health authorities.

The policy document notes that features of a truly integrated system of the CPA and care management would include:

- a single operational policy

- joint training for health and social care staff

- one lead officer for care co-ordination across health and social care

- common and agreed risk assessment and risk management processes

- a shared information system across health and social care

- a single complaints procedure

- agreement on the allocation of resources and, where possible, devolved budgets

- a joint serious incident process

- one point of access for health and social care assessments and co-ordinated health and social care.

Rationalisation of the CPA levels of need

The policy document identifies the characteristics of people on standard CPA:

- they require the support or intervention of one agency or discipline or they require only low key support from more than one agency or discipline

- they are more able to self-manage their mental health problems

- they have an active informal support network

- they pose little danger to themselves or others

- they are more likely to maintain appropriate contact with services

People on enhanced CPA are likely to have some of the following characteristics:

- multiple care needs, including housing, employment, etc., requiring inter-agency co-ordination

- only willing to co-operate with one professional or agency but have multiple care needs

- may be in contact with a number of agencies (including the criminal justice system)

- likely to require more frequent and intensive interventions, perhaps with medication management

- mental health problems coexisting with other problems, e.g. substance misuse

- they are more likely to be at risk of harming themselves or others

- they are more likely to disengage with services.

Role of the care co-ordinator

81. *The role of the care co-ordinator should usually be taken by the person who is best placed to oversee care planning and resource allocation. The care co-ordinator is responsible for keeping in close contact with the service user, and for advising the other members of the care team of changes in the circumstances of the service user which might require review or modification of the care plan. Where the user has standard needs and has contact with only one professional, whoever this may be, the role of the care co-ordinator should fall to this professional. The care co-ordinator is responsible for updating the service user's basic care plan and crisis plan.*

82. *It is critical that the care co-ordinator should have the authority to co-ordinate the delivery of the care plan and that this is respected by all those involved in*

> *delivering it, regardless of agency of origin. It is also critical that the care co-ordinator can understand and respond to the specific needs of the service user that may be related to their cultural or ethnic background.*

> 83. *Both health and social care managers should ensure that the care co-ordinator can combine the CPA care co-ordinator and care manager roles by having:*
>   - *competence in delivering mental health care (including an understanding of mental illness)*
>   - *knowledge of service user/family (including awareness of race, culture and gender issues)*
>   - *knowledge of community services and the role of other agencies;*
>   - *co-ordination skills*
>   - *access to resources.*

Chapter 10 of this guide includes extracts from current guidance on risk assessment of people being considered for hospital discharge. This includes material from the revised CPA policy as it refers to risk assessment, crisis and contingency planning.

National Service Framework

One of the government's aims in introducing the Mental Health National Service Framework was to introduce significant changes in the way mental health services are delivered so that people will value and use them and seek help earlier.

Standard 1 Health and social services should:

- promote mental health for all, working with individuals and communities

- combat discrimination against individuals and groups with mental health problems and promote their social inclusion.

Standard 2 Any service user who contacts their primary health care team with a common mental health problem should:

- have their mental health needs identified and assessed

- be offered effective treatments, including referral to specialist services for further assessment, treatment and care if they require it.

Standard 3 Any individual with a common mental health problem should:

- be able to make contact round the clock with the local services necessary to meet their needs and receive adequate care

- be able to use NHS Direct, as it develops, for first-level advice and referral on to specialist helplines or to local services.

Standard 4 All mental health service users on the CPA should:

- receive care which optimises engagement, prevents or anticipates crisis, and reduces risk

- have a copy of a written care plan which:

  - includes the action to be taken in a crisis by service users, their carers, and their care co-ordinators
  - advises the GP how they should respond if the service user needs additional help

– is regularly reviewed by the care co-ordinator

– be able to access services 24 hours a day, 365 days a year.

Standard 5 Each service user who is assessed as requiring a period of care away from their home should have:

- timely access to an appropriate hospital bed or alternative bed or place, which is:
  - in the least restrictive environment consistent with the need to protect them and the public
  - as close to home as possible

- a copy of a written after-care plan agreed on discharge, which sets out the care and rehabilitation to be provided, identifies the care co-ordinator, and specifies the action to be taken in a crisis.

Standard 6 All individuals who provide regular and substantial care for a period on CPA should:

- have an assessment of their caring, physical and mental health needs, repeated on a least an annual basis

- have their own written care plan, which is given to them and implemented in discussion with them.

Standard 7 Local health and social care communities should prevent suicides by:

- promoting mental health for all, working with individuals and communities (Standard 1)

- delivering high quality primary mental health care (Standard 2)

- ensuring that anyone with a mental health problem can contact local services via the primary care team, a helpline or an A&E department (Standard 3)

- ensuring that individuals with severe and enduring mental illness have a care plan which meets their specific needs, including access to services round the clock (Standard 4)

- providing safe hospital accommodation for individuals who need it (Standard 5)

- enabling individuals caring for someone with severe mental illness to receive the support which they need to continue to care (Standard 6)

and in addition:

- supporting local prison staff in preventing suicide among prisoners

- ensuring that staff are competent to assess the risk of suicide among individuals at greatest risk

- developing local systems for suicide audit to learn lessons and take any necessary action.

Links between supervised after-care and the CPA

Section 25A only applies to some patients subject to s117 after-care (i.e. those on ss3,37,47 or 48). A larger group of detained patients will be on enhanced CPA. See Figure 2.2. The diagrams can be viewed in various ways:

- If you move from left to right you may develop a mental disorder (column 1) and find yourself subject to CPA (column 2). You may have multiple needs or be seen as a risk to self or others and be placed on enhanced CPA (column 3). If you are then detained under the Mental Health Act, certain sections have the benefit of being subject to statutory after-care (see columns 4 and 5) and finally, of this group, some will be made subject to supervised after-care when discharged (column 6).

- If you then look back from right to left you see section 25A is based on section 117 after-care, which should now be based on local CPA arrangements. Thus, based on the CPA an individual should have a clear care plan which is, in effect, their section 117 plan to be attached to the section 25A documentation.

- The dotted lines indicate moves from one stage to another. Apart from the left-to-right movement it is also possible to move from some detention sections to others (e.g. 2 to 3).

The diagram is a visual aid to understanding. It is not to scale (e.g. the proportion of those detained who go on to supervised after-care) nor is it claimed to be an accurate map of movements between different parts of the system. It is designed to show the importance of basing section 25A on CPA and section 117.

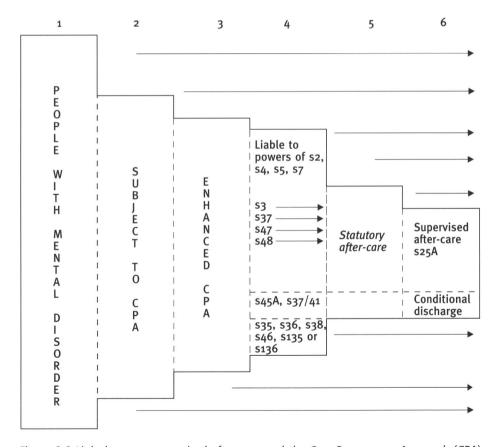

Figure 2.2 Links between supervised after-care and the Care Programme Approach (CPA)

Activity 2.1

Sample questions on Part II of the Mental Health Act 1983

1a *What are the main grounds which need to exist before a doctor can recommend that a person should be detained in hospital for assessment under section 2 of the Act?*

1b *How does the expression 'dangerous to other persons or himself' compare with these grounds and what is its significance?*

1c *If the dangerousness test was considered to apply, how might an ASW then become involved?*

2a *Who may grant leave to a patient detained on section 3?*

2b *What should this person do in granting leave and what conditions can be imposed?*

2c *When do you think it might be seen as justifiable for a patient to be kept subject to section 17 leave for a long period rather than being placed on supervised after-care?*

Chapter 3
Relatives and carers

The nearest relative under the Mental Health Act 1983

Introduction

The nearest relative has a number of important rights and functions under the Act. These are discussed later and include the right to:

- insist on an ASW's assessment of the need for a person's detention in hospital

- be consulted where practicable* before a section 3 is applied for (and in effect block it)

- apply for a person's detention in hospital

- order the patient's discharge.

* 'where practicable' has been defined in a way which gives the ASW a fair degree of flexibility in *R (E)* v *Bristol* [2005]

The first problem is to identify who exactly is the nearest relative. It will not necessarily be the person identified by the patient as their next of kin and, indeed, the patient has little control over who will be seen in law as the nearest relative. It is worth noting that in *Re. D* (*Mental patient: Habeas corpus*, Court of Appeal, 2000) the judge stated: 'the question the court had to consider in deciding whether the application for detention had been validly made was not whether the social worker consulted with the legally correct nearest relative, but whether the patient's daughter appeared to him to be the correct relative'.

Section 26 provides a list of people considered to be relatives under the Act. Being a relative is of itself important as ASWs should have regard to any wishes they express (see s13(1)); it may enable them to apply to County Court for ruling on a nearest relative issue (see later in the chapter); and being such a relative is a pre-requisite to being nearest relative (apart from where the court intervenes or where powers are transferred under Regulation 14).

Complications concerning children and 'the five-year rule' (whereby people in some settings find another resident may become their nearest relative) are discussed later. What follows here is a quick guide to enable an ASW to make a reasonable decision in identifying the nearest relative.

Disagreements or mistakes in identifying a nearest relative

There have been some problems where the ASW or the hospital managers decide after an admission that the wrong person has been identified as the nearest relative. There are different views as to the correct way to respond to this situation and in such a case staff would be well advised to seek a view from their solicitor.

In a judicial review (*R* v *MHRT for West Midlands and North West ex parte* H) (2000) it was held that restricted patients do not have a nearest relative. This is because there is no legal function for a nearest relative for such a patient. When compiling reports for Mental Health Review Tribunals it is important, therefore, not to refer to anyone as the nearest relative.

Route to the nearest relative

To identify a person's nearest relative go through the following four stages:

1 Make a list of any of the following who are ordinarily resident in the UK, the Channel Islands or Isle of Man. (This assumes the patient is ordinarily so resident. If not, then the nearest relative may be someone who is, similarly, not so resident.) That is, list the patient's:

- Husband or wife
  - (a) unless permanently separated from the patient by agreement or by a court order, or where one partner has deserted the other;
  - (b) may be someone who has lived as husband or wife* for the last six months or more if patient not legally married, or patient is married but (a) applies.
- Son or daughter
- Father or mother
- Brother or sister
- Grandparent
- Grandchild
- Uncle or aunt
- Nephew or niece
- Any other person with whom the patient has ordinarily resided for five years or more.

In compiling the list, include half-blood relationships, treat illegitimate children as the legitimate children of their mothers, and do not include in-law relationships.

2 Cross out anyone under the age of 18 unless they are the patient's spouse or parent.

3 Highlight anyone on the list who ordinarily resides with or cares for the patient (or did so before the patient was admitted to hospital). 'Caring for' ** is a matter of judgement and could include shopping, cooking or providing other care. If only one person is highlighted, they are the nearest relative. If more than one person is highlighted (or no one), then go to the next stage.

4 Ranking in order of priority. If more than one person was highlighted above in stage 3, then rank only those who were highlighted. If no one was highlighted, the ranking applies to everyone on the list. The person highest in the list in stage 1 is the nearest relative. If there is more than one person in the same category, then whole-blood relatives are preferred to half-blood and elder is preferred to younger.

* As a result of *R* v *Liverpool* (2002) this could be a same-sex relationship. However, the introduction of Civil Partnerships in 2005 did not alter the Mental Health Act so same-sex partnerships still need to be for six months. In 2006 the government announced plans to amend this.

** In *re D* (*Mental patient: Habeas corpus*) (Court of Appeal, 2000) the judge stated that 'the words ''cared for'' were not defined in the Act but they were clear everyday words set in the context where a social worker had to act in a common sense manner'. The word 'ordinarily' in s4 applied to 'residing with' and not to 'caring', so a person may only recently have started providing the care. See also under 'Carers' legislation' below.

Discussion points

1 *The Children Act 1989*

It is unusual for children under 18 to be detained under the Mental Health Act. There is a lower age limit of 16 for guardianship but there is no lower age limit for detention. In cases where admission is considered, the nearest relative will usually be the older parent. If a child is living with a person under a residence order within the meaning of the Children Act, then that person will be the nearest relative. If a local authority has parental responsibility under a care order, then it will be the nearest relative. In those rare cases where the child is a ward of court, no application for detention may be made without the court's leave. Chapter 31 of the Code of Practice to the Mental Health Act 1983 gives some specific advice on children and young people under the age of 18.

2 *'The Five-Year rule'*

The Act introduced a new category of persons to be treated as if they are relatives. These are defined in section 26(7) as persons with whom the patient has been 'ordinarily residing for a period of not less than five years'. Together with the preference in section 26(4) for making the nearest relative the person whom 'the patient ordinarily resides with or is cared for by', this has created some strange situations in practice. Consider the situation of a patient who has lived in an old-people's home with the same group of people for more than five years. If they eat together and share common facilities, they should probably be included within the meaning of 'the patient ordinarily resides with'. Assuming none of the other residents is a blood relative, the eldest of them will probably be nearest relative. This will apply even if the patient has blood relatives elsewhere, unless one is 'caring for' the patient. In a recent publication, Eldergill takes a different view and argues that this would only apply if the person had voluntarily chosen to live with a specific person. 'There must be some element of choice before a person may be said to ordinarily reside with another' (Eldergill 1998, p103). There is room for debate.

3 *Patient objects to nearest relative – European Convention on Human Rights*

The Act requires an ASW to consult with the nearest relative where practicable but this poses a problem where the patient objects to contact (e.g. where there has been abuse) on the grounds that it violates their human rights. Article 8 states everyone has a right to respect for their private and family life, their home and correspondence. ASWs may wish to seek advice where the patient would not want the nearest relative contacted because it would cause distress. The MHA Commission Biennial Report 1999–2001 equates 'practicable' with possible, but see

Jones' comments (2004, pp. 81–83) on the definition of 'practicable' in contacting a nearest relative.

In the case of *JT* v *UK* (2000), JT was detained under section 3. She was moved to a secure unit in November 1984 and to a special hospital in 1987. Her detention was subject to periodic review by MHRTs and she was discharged in January 1996. JT complained to the Commission that she had been unable to change her nearest relative, in violation of Article 8. Her nearest relative was her mother with whom she had had a difficult relationship. JT had wanted to nominate another person, so personal information, mainly in relation to MHRTs, was not released to her mother, or to her stepfather (against whom the applicant had made allegations of sexual abuse). The Commission declared admissible the complaint under Article 8 para. 1 concerning her inability to change her nearest relative during her period of detention. The case was struck out by the European Court of Human Rights after a friendly settlement was reached: the UK government agreed to amend the law to allow a detainee to apply to the County Court to have a nearest relative replaced if the patient reasonably objected to that person acting in that capacity (Times Law Report 0504-2000, see Chapter 11). With the delay in the new Mental Health Bill there is concern that this problem has still not been addressed in statute. There has been some discussion of a possible remedial order but in the meantime the High Court *R* v *Bristol* case [2005] EWHC 74 (Admin) has been supportive of Jones' view on 'practicability' influenced by the point made above on European Convention Article 8. In the Bristol case it was ruled that the ASW had discretion to decide not to consult the nearest relative of a competent patient who objected and whose psychiatrist said such consultation would be detrimental to the patient's health. ASWs may need to seek further advice on specific cases.

Changing or displacing the nearest relative

If mentally competent, a nearest relative may authorise someone else to perform their functions under Regulation 14 of the Mental Health (Hospital, Guardianship and Consent to Treatment) Regulations 1983. This other person need not be a relative as defined by the Act but they must not be in one of the categories (such as persons under the age of 18) excluded under section 26(5). The authorisation needs to be in writing and copies lodged with the person authorised and with the hospital managers (for detained patients) or the local authority (for guardianship). This procedure may be useful in the circumstances outlined above (where the eldest resident could authorise a suitable relative) or in any other cases where both parties are agreeable. This might be where those involved do not feel that the legal nearest relative is the right person to carry out that function. Strictly speaking, the patient does not have a say in this, which seems unfortunate. (See below for sample form.)

Second, there are some circumstances (e.g. where the nearest relative of the patient is not capable of acting as such by reason of mental disorder) where this is not the appropriate action and where an application to the County Court is needed. The court may direct someone to carry out nearest relative's functions on application from:

(a) any relative of the patient

(b) any other person with whom the patient is residing (or if the patient is then an in-patient in a hospital, was last residing before he was admitted)

(c) an approved social worker.

The grounds for an application are set out in section 29(3):

(a)   that the patient has no nearest relative within the meaning of this Act, or that it is not reasonably practicable to ascertain whether he has such a relative, or who that relative is

(b)   that the nearest relative of the patient is incapable of acting as such by reason of mental disorder or other illness

(c)   that the nearest relative of the patient unreasonably objects to the making of an application for admission for treatment or a guardianship application in respect of the patient

(d)   that the nearest relative of the patient has exercised without due regard to the welfare of the patient or the interests of the public his power to discharge the patient from hospital or guardianship under this Part of this Act, or is likely to do so.

Where (c) or (d) apply, and the patient is already detained under section 2, the detention will last until the Court reaches a decision. If the decision is to make an order giving someone else the functions of the nearest relative, there is a further seven-day period which would allow a section 3 assessment form to be completed. Where (a) or (b) are the grounds the Court can specify a time limit for the order. If (c) or (d) obtains or where no time limit is set under (a) or (b), the order lasts until the patient is no longer liable to detention or subject to guardianship.

Rights and functions of the nearest relative and their relationship with the ASW

(i)   The nearest relative is able to be the applicant for detentions in hospital under sections 2, 3 and 4 and for guardianship under section 7. The Code of Practice states:

> *2.35 The ASW is usually the right applicant, bearing in mind professional training, knowledge of the legislation and of local resources, together with the potentially adverse effect that an application by the nearest relative might have on the latter's relationship with the patient. The doctor should therefore advise the nearest relative that it is preferable for an ASW to make an assessment of the need for a patient to be admitted under the Act, and for the ASW to make the application. When reasonably practicable, the doctor should, however, advise the nearest relative of the rights set out in Section 13(4) and of his or her right to make an application.*

> *2.36 The doctor should never advise the nearest relative to make the application in order to avoid involving an ASW in an assessment.*

There has been some debate concerning the nearest relative as applicant, especially where the ASW believes that an application would not be appropriate.

The Code of Practice states at para. 2.32:

> *The ASW must discuss with the patient's nearest relative the reasons for not making an application and should advise the nearest relative of his or her right to do this. If the nearest relative wishes to pursue this the ASW should suggest that he or she consult with the Doctors.*

It would probably be good practice for an ASW to explain these rights as early as possible in the assessment process. It might cause confusion and difficulty if this were left until the last moment in a case where an ASW decided not to make an application. Indeed, Jones (2004, p. 665) states:

> *The use of the mandatory term 'must' is unfortunate in this context. Giving reasons to a nearest relative for not making an application is only a legal requirement in the circumstances set out in s13(4). As the imparting of information to a nearest relative about the patient's situation is a breach of the patient's right to respect for his private life under Art8(1) of the European Convention of Human Rights, a justification for taking such action must be found in Art 8(2).*

(ii)   Where the nearest relative is the applicant

Section 14 requires a social worker to provide a social circumstances report to the hospital. If this social worker happens to be an ASW who has earlier refused to make an application, Jones (2004, p. 101) is of the opinion that the report should include an account of the reasons for this. Presumably, in cases where an ASW thought that compulsory admission was inappropriate, they would already have made the reasons clear to the nearest relative and to the doctors involved and possibly to the hospital managers.

(iii)   Assistance with escorting the patient to hospital.

The Code of Practice states:

> *11.8 If an ASW is the applicant, he or she has a professional responsibility for ensuring that all necessary arrangements are made for the patient to be conveyed to hospital.*

> *11.9 If the nearest relative is the applicant, the assistance of an ASW should be made available if requested. If this is not possible, other professionals involved in the admission should give advice and assistance.*

(iv)   Section 11(3) requires the ASW to 'take such steps as are practicable' to explain to the nearest relative 'before or within a reasonable time after an application for the admission of a patient for assessment' that an application is being, or has been, made and of their rights to discharge a patient under section 23. In exercising this power, the nearest relative must give the hospital managers 72 hours' written notice of their intention. It would be advisable for the ASW to explain that the responsible medical officer (RMO) may block this discharge if able to produce within the 72 hours 'a report certifying that in the opinion of that officer, the patient, if discharged, would be likely to act in a manner dangerous to other persons or to himself'.

(See chart of risk criteria under 'two-stage approach to a Mental Health assessment' in Chapter 2.)

(v)   Where an ASW is unable to meet the above requirement to notify the nearest relative before admission, the Code (2.15) states they 'should notify the hospital as soon as this has been done'. ASWs should ensure they persist with efforts to contact the NR after an admission, subject to any Article 8 concerns.

(vi)   The right to object. The ASW must not make an application for the detention of a patient under section 3 or for guardianship under section 7 if the nearest relative objects. Under the provisions of section 11(4) the ASW must consult with the nearest relative before making such an application 'unless it appears to that social worker that in the circumstances such consultation is not reasonably practicable or would involve unreasonable delay'. (see discussion re: Article 8 above).

(vii)   The right to an assessment

Under Section 13(4) it is:

> *the duty of a local social services authority, if so required by the nearest relative of a patient residing in their area, to direct an approved social worker as soon as practicable to take the patient's case into consideration ... with a view to making an application for his admission to hospital; and if in any such case that approved social worker decides not to make an application he shall inform the nearest relative of his reasons in writing.*

Para. 2.32 of the Code states:

> *Such a letter should contain sufficient details to enable the nearest relative to understand the decision whilst at the same time preserving the patient's right to confidentiality.*

The Code of Practice indicates that authorities should issue ASWs with guidance on what would constitute such a request from a nearest relative and whether they should include referrals routed via GPs or other professionals.

(viii) Section 133 requires hospitals to give the nearest relative seven days' notice of the intended discharge of a detained patient unless the patient or nearest relative has asked for this information not to be given. This appears to be a much-ignored part of the Act which adds fuel to the fire of some relatives' arguments that they are not kept properly informed.

(ix)   Apart from these statutory duties the Code (2.14) also advises ASWs to:

a.   *ascertain the nearest relative's views about both the patient's needs and the relative's own needs in relation to the patient*

b.   *inform the nearest relative of the reasons for considering an application for admission under the Mental Health Act and the effects of making an application.*

Quick route to the nearest relative – example of documentation

(This could be expanded or included within other documentation.)
Insert brief details of any of the following who are ordinarily resident in the UK, Channel Islands or Isle of Man (assuming the patient is ordinarily so resident; if not, the nearest relative may be someone who is, similarly, not so resident). Ensure that anyone who qualifies for the list and who is living with or caring for the patient, is included.

In compiling the list, include half-blood relationships, treat illegitimate children as the legitimate children of their mothers, and do not include in-law relationships.

If only one person is ticked in both of the final two columns then they are the nearest relative.

Ranking in order of priority. If more than one person is ticked, the nearest relative is the highest of those listed. If no one was so ticked, the ranking applies to everyone on the list. If there is more than one person in a category, whole-blood relatives are preferred to half-blood, elder is preferred to younger.

Relationship Where there is more than one person in a category underline the eldest	Name and contact address or telephone number wherever this might be useful	One tick for each person in category	Tick if 18 or over. Insert age if under 18	Tick if living with or caring** for patient at point of assessment or at time of admission to hospital/ guardianship
Husband or wife* May include someone who has lived as if husband and wife for the last six months or more.				
Son or daughter				
Father or mother				
Brother or sister				
Grandparent				
Grandchild				
Uncle or aunt				
Nephew or niece				
Five-year rule Person with whom patient has ordinarily resided for five years or more				

*   unless permanently separated by agreement or court order or where a partner has deserted the other

**   'Caring for' is a matter of ASW judgement but should usually be substantial and sustained.

Suggested documentation for Regulation 14

To use this form you need to be sure that (i) the first person named is indeed the nearest relative, and (ii) they are not incapable of acting as such through reasons of mental disorder or other illness.

Letter from the Nearest Relative under the Mental Health Act 1983 delegating the functions to another person under Regulation 14 of the Mental Health Act (Hospital, Guardianship and Consent to Treatment) Regulations 1983.

I (full name) ....

of (address) ....

....

(telephone no.) ....

being the nearest relative of ....

as (state relationship to patient) ....

within the meaning of the Mental Health Act 1983, hereby authorise

(full name) ....

of (address) ....

....

(telephone no.) ....

(state relationship to patient) ....

to perform in respect of the patient the functions conferred upon the nearest relative by Part II of the Mental Health Act 1983 of the associated Regulations.

This authorisation is to last: ☐ until further notice

(please tick one box) ☐ or until.. (specify date)

☐ until the end of the current detention/guardianship

I understand that I may revoke this authority at any time (despite whichever box I have ticked above) by giving notice in writing to the person authorised and
(a) in the case of hospital detention, the hospital managers, or
(b) in the case of guardianship, the local authority and private guardian (if any).

I agree to a copy of this letter being passed to the person authorised, the hospital managers and, in the case of guardianship, the local authority and private guardian, to act as a notice of my delegation of nearest relative functions under the Mental Health Act 1983 and associated Regulations.

(to be signed by donor):
Signed .... Date ....

I acknowledge receipt of this authorisation to act as nearest relative as detailed above
(to be signed by recipient):

Carers' legislation [Carers (Recognition and Services) Act 1995]

Introduction

This legislation began as a Private Member's Bill. It received government support at its second reading but was significantly amended at committee stage. Its sponsor, Mr Malcolm Wicks MP, described its purpose as follows: 'It is crucial to ensure that local authorities take proper account of carers' circumstances when carrying out an assessment of the need for community care services of the person being cared for.' Based on the general household survey, Wicks considered that there were something in the region of 6.8 million carers in Britain. An estimated 1.5 million carers provide care for 20 hours a week or more.

The main provisions of the Act

Section 1 is the key provision for England and Wales and is set out in full below.

Assessment of ability of carers to provide care: England and Wales.

(1) *Subject to subsection (3) below, in any case where –*

   (a) *a local authority carry out an assessment under section 47(1)(a) of the National Health Service and Community Care Act 1990 of the needs of a person ('relevant person') for community care services and*

   (b) *an individual ('the carer') provides or intends to provide a substantial amount of care on a regular basis for the relevant person the carer may request the local authority, before they make their decision as to whether the needs of the relevant person call for the provision of any services, to carry out an assessment of his ability to provide and to continue to provide care for the relevant person; and if he makes such a request, the local authority shall carry out such an assessment and shall take into account the results of that assessment in making that decision.*

(2) *Subject to subsection (3) below, in any case where –*

   (a) *a local authority assess the needs of a disabled child for the purposes of Part III of the Children Act 1989 or section 2 of the Chronically Sick and Disabled Persons Act 1970, and*

   (b) *an individual ('the carer') provides or intends to provide a substantial amount of care on a regular basis for the disabled child, the carer may request the local authority, before they make their decision as to whether the needs of the disabled child call for the provision of any services, to carry out an assessment of his ability to provide and to continue to provide care for the disabled child, and if he makes such a request, the local authority shall carry out such an assessment and shall take into account the results of that assessment in writing that decision,*

(3) *No request may be made under subsection (1) or (2) above by an individual who provides or will provide the care in question –*

   (a) *by virtue of a contract of employment or other contract with any person; or*

   (b) *as a volunteer for a voluntary organisation.*

(4) The Secretary of State may give directions as to the manner in which an assessment under subsection (1) or (2) above is to be carried out or the form it is to take but, subject to any such directions, it shall be carried out in such manner and take such form as the local authority consider appropriate.

(5) Section 8 of the Disabled Persons (Services, Consultation and Representation) Act 1986 (duty of local authority to take into account ability of carers) shall not apply in any case where –

(a) an assessment is made under subsection (1) above in respect of an individual who provides the care in question for a disabled person; or

(b) an assessment is made under subjection (2) above.

(6) In this section –

'community care services' has the meaning given by section 46(3) of the National Health Service and Community Care Act 1990;

'child' means a person under the age of eighteen.

'disabled child' means a child who is disabled within the meaning of Part III of the Children Act 1989;

'disabled person' means a person to whom section 29 of the National Assistance Act 1948 applies;

'local authority' has the meaning given by section 46(3) of the National Health Service and Community Care Act 1990; and

'voluntary organisation' has the same meaning as in the National Assistance Act 1948.

Notes on the Act:

-   'Assessment' would include re-assessment.

-   The phrase 'intends to provide' may have particular relevance when assessing the situation before someone is discharged from hospital.

-   'Substantial amount of care on a regular basis' can be seen as linking with section 26(4) of the Mental Health Act 1983 in some circumstances (e.g. the issue of a carer taking priority over other relatives when trying to determine who is the nearest relative). In *re D (Mental patient: Habeas corpus)* (Court of Appeal, 9 May 2000) the judge stated:

    the words 'cared for' were not defined in the Act but they were clear everyday words set in the context where a social worker had to act in a common sense manner in a very difficult situation. The [original] judge had been correct in declining to supplement the language of the section. The amount of care provided was more than minimal even though it fell short of long-term care of the kind envisaged in s1 (b) of the Carers (Recognition and Services) Act 1995.

-   Paid carers or those acting for voluntary organisations are excluded from these provisions.

-   Children are included and may need to be encouraged to make requests so assessments of their ability to provide care are formally made.

Carers and Disabled Children Act 2000

This legislation allows local authorities to provide services and support directly to carers. This can include direct payments. A carer's own needs can now be directly assessed. The Act also introduced a short-term break voucher scheme designed to provide flexibility in the timing of carers' breaks. Any services to carers may be subject to a charge.

Section 2 of the Act requires a local authority to carry out an assessment of a person aged 16 or over who informally provides or intends to provide a substantial amount of care on a regular basis for someone aged 18 or over if that person asks the authority to assess their ability to do so.

Other relevant legislation

Chapter 9 looks at a range of other legislation which might be relevant. For example, section 8 of the Disabled Persons (Services, Consultation and Representation) Act 1986 requires the local authority to have regard to the ability of a carer to provide to the disabled person ('disabled person' includes people with a mental disorder).

Schedule 8 of the NHS Act 1977 and section 111 of the Local Government Act 1972 enable social services departments to provide facilities such as information and carers' support groups without having to be asked for an assessment.

Activity 3.1

Sample questions on relatives and carers

1a You are an ASW and have determined the identity of a patient's nearest relative. You have decided an application under section 2 is appropriate. According to the Mental Health Act and Code, what should you do with regard to the nearest relative?

1b From an early stage the patient makes it clear that they object to you speaking to the nearest relative and that, if detained, they will block the hospital from making contact with the nearest relative. Why is the Human Rights Act 1998 relevant here?

2a Who can apply to the County Court for the appointment of a nearest relative?

2b In what ways does this potentially engage any specific Articles of the European Convention on Human Rights?

2c What arguments might be put for or against seeking a nearest relative for someone who does not seem to have one at the point of assessing for a section 3 admission?

Chapter 4
The role of the approved social worker

Tasks for ASWs involved in assessments under the Mental Health Act

This can form the basis of an exercise near the beginning of an ASW course. Task: identify the legal basis of these requirements and discuss their meaning; note down section numbers (from Act) or paragraphs (Code of Practice or the Memorandum).

1   To interview the patient in a 'suitable manner'.

2   To have 'regard to any wishes expressed by relatives'.

3   Consider 'all the circumstances of the case', including: past history of the patient's mental disorder, the patient's present condition, social, family and personal factors, the wishes of the patient and their relatives, medical opinion.

4   Consider: informal admission, day care, out-patient treatment, community psychiatric nursing support, crisis intervention centres, primary health care support, local authority social services provision, support from friends, relatives, voluntary agencies.

5   Decide whether 'detention in a hospital is in all the circumstances of the case the most appropriate way of providing the care and medical treatment of which the patient stands in need'.

6   Ensure that it is 'necessary or proper for the application to be made by' the ASW.

7   Take such steps as are practicable to inform the nearest relative that an application has been, or is about to be made and inform them of their powers of discharge under section 23.

8 (If considering section 3) ensure that the nearest relative does not object to the application being made.

9 To convey the patient to hospital if an application is made by the ASW (with the powers of a constable).

10 If the ASW has been unable to inform the nearest relative before the patient's admission, he or she should notify the hospital as soon as this has been done.

11 If the patient is admitted, the ASW should make sure that any moveable property of the patient is protected.

12 If the nearest relative applies for section 2 or 3, a social worker must 'interview the patient and produce a report on his social circumstances' for the hospital managers.

13 If required to do so by the nearest relative, the SSD must direct an ASW to assess whether to make an application for detention. If the ASW does not apply, they must give their reasons in writing to the nearest relative.

14 Leave an outline report at the hospital when the patient is admitted, giving reasons for the admission and any practical matters that the hospital should know.

Assessment for possible compulsory admission or guardianship

The key professionals in assessing a person's need for possible compulsory admission to hospital, or for guardianship, are two doctors and an approved social worker. Although the nearest relative may apply for detention, the Code of Practice states at para. 2.35 that the ASW is usually the right applicant. In practice, nearest relative applications are rare. The Mental Health Act 1983 sets out the criteria which must be satisfied before a person can be detained. These have already been considered in Chapter 2 of this guide. This chapter will consider the process of assessment and the guidance contained in the Code of Practice. Chapter 2 of the Code of Practice covers assessment for possible admission. Although it makes some reference to guardianship there is also further guidance on this in Chapter 13 of the Code. Chapter 2 of the Code was redrafted to bring together the material on professional communication as this was seen as central to the process of assessment.

> 2.3 *Doctors and ASWs undertaking assessments need to apply professional judgement, and reach decisions, independently of each other but in a framework of co-operation and mutual support. Good working relationships require knowledge and understanding by the members of each profession of the other's distinct role and responsibilities. Unless there are good reasons for undertaking separate assessments, assessments should be carried out jointly by the ASW and doctor(s). It is essential that at least one of the doctors undertaking the medical assessment discusses the patient with the applicant (ASW or nearest relative) and it is desirable for both of them to do this.*

> 2.4 *Everyone involved in assessment should be alert to the need to provide support for colleagues, especially where there is a risk of the patient causing physical harm. Staff should be aware of circumstances where the police should be called to provide assistance, and how to use that assistance to minimise the risk of violence.*

Paragraph 2.6 considers the statutory criteria which need to be satisfied before a patient is admitted under Part II of the Act but it also sets out a number of other factors which should be taken into consideration when making an assessment. These are:

- the guiding principles in Chapter 1
- the patient's wishes and view of his or her own needs
- the patient's social and family circumstances
- the nature of the illness/behaviour disorder and its course
- what may be known about the patient by his or her nearest relative, and other relatives or friends and professionals involved, assessing in particular how reliable this information is
- other forms of care or treatment including, where relevant, consideration of whether the patient would be willing to accept medical treatment in hospital informally or as an out-patient and of whether guardianship would be appropriate
- the needs of the patient's family or others with whom he or she lives
- the need for others to be protected from the patient
- the burden on those close to the patient of a decision not to admit under the Act.

There are several guiding principles at para. 1.1 including advice that people should:

- be given respect for their qualities, abilities and diverse backgrounds as individuals and be assured that account will be taken of their age, gender, sexual orientation, social, cultural and religious background, but that general assumptions will not be made on the basis of any one of these characteristics
- have their needs taken fully into account, though it is recognised that, within available resources, it may not always be practicable to meet them in full
- be given any necessary treatment or care in the least controlled and segregated facilities compatible with ensuring their own health or safety or the safety of other people
- be discharged from detention or other powers provided by the Act as soon as it is clear that their application is no longer justified.

Interpreters

Paragraph 1.4 states:

> *Local and Health Authorities and Trusts should ensure that ASWs, Doctors, Nurses and others receive sufficient guidance in the use of interpreters and should make arrangements for there to be an easily accessible pool of trained interpreters. Authorities and Trusts should consider co-operating in making this provision.*

Section 13(2) of the Act requires the ASW to interview the patient in a 'suitable manner' and paragraph 2.12 of the Code gives some detailed guidance on this. The Code balances the need for a full assessment with the risks to the worker, patient and others.

The guidance in the Code involving the nearest relative was revised to take into account case experiences under the Act. This includes:

> *2.14*
> *The ASW must attempt to identify the patient's nearest relative as defined in section 26 of the Act ...*

It is important to remember that the nearest relative for the purposes of the Act may not be the same person as the patient's 'next of kin' and also that the identity of the nearest relative is liable to change with the passage of time. The ASW must then ensure that the statutory obligations to the nearest relative set out in section 11 of the Act are fulfilled. In addition, the ASW should where possible:

a. *ascertain the nearest relative's views about both the patient's needs and the relative's own needs in relation to the patient*
b. *inform the nearest relative of the reasons for considering an application for admission under the Mental Health Act and the effects of making such an application*

2.15

It is a statutory requirement to take such steps as are practicable to inform the nearest relative about an application for admission under section 2 and of their power of discharge (section 11(3)). If the ASW has been unable to inform the nearest relative before the patient's admission, he or she should notify the hospital as soon as this has been done.

2.16

Consultation by the ASW with the nearest relative about possible application for admission under section 3 or reception into guardianship is a statutory requirement unless it is not reasonably practicable or would involve unreasonable delay (section 11(4)). Circumstances in which the nearest relative need not be informed or consulted include those where the ASW cannot obtain sufficient information to establish the identity or location of the nearest relative or where to do so would require an excessive amount of investigation. Practicability* refers to the availability of the nearest relative and not to the appropriateness of informing or consulting the person concerned. If the ASW has been unable to consult the nearest relative before making an application for admission for treatment (section 3) he or she should persist in seeking to contact the nearest relative so as to inform the latter of his or her powers to discharge the patient under section 23. The ASW should inform the hospital as soon as this has been done.

See Chapter 3 on relatives to see how this might not be seen as a correct view.

Delegation of nearest relative's functions

2.17

If the nearest relative would find it difficult to undertake the functions defined in the Act or is reluctant for any reason to do this Regulation 14 allows him or her to delegate those functions to another person. ASWs should consider proposing this in appropriate cases.

Paragraph 2.21 notes that when the ASW has reached a decision, they should inform (with reasons):

- the patient
- the patient's nearest relative (whenever practicable)
- the doctor(s) involved in the assessment
- the key worker, if the patient is on CPA

- the patient's GP, if he or she was not involved in the assessment.

When a patient has been taken to a place of safety under section 136 of the Act, the assessment by an ASW and doctor should begin as soon as possible after arrival at the place of safety. Local policies should set target times for the commencement of the assessment.

The Appendices to this *Guide* provide ASWs with checklists for assessments under sections 2, 3, 4 and 7 to ensure that all necessary actions have been taken. These should be read in conjunction with any local procedures.

ASW responsibility for actions and section 139

There are a number of myths concerning the ASW's position in terms of responsibility for actions that they take under the Mental Health Act. For example, some people seem to consider that ASWs are acting as free agents and that their employing authorities have no responsibility for their actions. Jones clarifies the position when he considers the ASW's position when deciding whether or not to make an application as per section 13 of the Act:

> *The duty is placed on the approved social worker and not on his employing authority (*Nottingham City Council *v* Unison *[2004] EWHC893, para 18). An approved social worker is therefore personally liable for his actions when carrying out functions under this Act. He or she should exercise his or her own judgement, based upon social and medical evidence, and not act at the behest of the local authority, medical practitioners or other persons who might be involved with the patient's welfare.* (Jones, 2004, p. 94)

Jones is also of the opinion that the ASW owes a duty of care to people they are assessing for possible admission under the Act. ASWs should record the reasons for their decisions concerning applications. The general role of ASWs and how they are integrated within a mental health service is considered in the next part of the *Guide* that looks at the management and supervision of approved social workers.

Section 139 of the Mental Health Act is of importance when considering the liability of an ASW for actions taken in relation to the Act:

> *139(1) No person shall be liable, whether on the grounds of want of jurisdiction or any other ground, to any civil or criminal proceedings to which he would have been liable apart from this section in respect of any act purporting to be done in pursuance of this Act or any regulations or rules made under this Act, or in pursuance of anything done in the discharge of functions conferred by any other enactment on the authority having jurisdiction under Part VII of this Act, unless the act was done in bad faith or without reasonable care.*

> *(2) No civil proceedings shall be brought against any person in any court in respect of any such act without the leave of the High Court; and no criminal proceedings shall be brought against any person in any court in respect of any such act except by or with the consent of the Director of Public Prosecutions.*

This does not prevent the patient from applying to the High Court for a writ of habeas corpus so that the lawfulness of the detention can be tested.

Whether a person has acted in bad faith or without reasonable care is a question of fact with the burden of proof lying with the applicant. The relevance of the Code of Practice to any action against an ASW can be seen in the introduction to the Code that states:

> *The Act does not impose a legal duty to comply with the Code but, as it is a statutory document, failure to follow it could be referred to in evidence in legal proceedings*

A positive note for ASWs and employers is made by Jones (2004, p. 420):

> *Although an approved social worker acts in a personal capacity ... as an employee he or she will be protected by the doctrine of vicarious liability and the local authority will be liable for wrongs done while acting in the course of his or her employment ... A legal action brought against either an approved social worker or his employing authority will succeed only if evidence of bad faith or lack of reasonable care is present (s139).*

Hoggett (1996, p250) takes a critical stance on section 139 when she states that:

> *There is no necessary connection between vexatiousness and the use of compulsion under the Mental Health Act. There is no evidence that the floodgates would open if section 139 were entirely repealed. There is more evidence, from a series of reports and investigations, that mental patients are in a peculiarly powerless position which merits, if anything, extra safeguards rather than the removal of those available to everyone else.*

To act in good faith and reasonable care I would suggest that an ASW needs to be 'angst-ridden but strangely decisive', i.e. concerned to respect a person's right to freedom but prepared to intervene decisively where the level of mental disorder and risk requires it.

The importance of the ASW role was stated by Lord Bingham in the House of Lords judgement on the Von Brandenburg case when he said: 'I would, secondly, resist the lumping together of the ASW and the recommending doctor or doctors as "the mental health professionals". It is the ASW who makes the application, not the doctors.'

The question being raised was: 'When a mental health review tribunal has ordered the discharge of a patient, is it lawful to readmit him under section 2 or section 3 of the [Mental Health Act 1983] where it cannot be demonstrated that there has been a relevant change of circumstances?' The outcome was essentially that an ASW must not fly in the face of a tribunal decision of which they are aware:

> *an ASW may not lawfully apply for the admission of a patient whose discharge has been ordered by the decision of a mental health review tribunal of which the ASW is aware unless the ASW has formed the reasonable and bona fide opinion that he has information not known to the tribunal which puts a significantly different complexion on the case as compared with that which was before the tribunal.*
> (R *v* East London and the City Mental Health NHS Trust and another (Respondents) ex parte von Brandenburg *(2003))*

Management and supervision of approved social workers

This part of the chapter gives details of some key issues involved in the management and supervision of ASWs. It places the role of the approved social worker in context and clarifies which tasks can only be performed by an ASW. It also lists tasks that they are likely to be involved in, but which can also be performed by other staff.

Statutory basis for employing ASWs

Section 114 of the Mental Health Act 1983 states the following:

(1) *A local social services authority shall appoint a sufficient number of approved social workers for the purpose of discharging the functions conferred on them by this Act.*

(2) *No person shall be appointed by a local social services authority as an approved social worker unless he is approved by the authority as having appropriate competence in dealing with persons who are suffering from mental disorder.*

(3) *In approving a person for appointment as an approved social worker a local social services Authority shall have regard to such matters as the Secretary of State may direct.*

The relevant circular, containing the Secretary of State's directions, is DHSS Circular Number LAC(86)15 (titled: *Mental Health Act 1983 – Approved Social Workers*). CCETSW's exercise of its powers given to it by the Secretary of State were initially set out in the Paper 19:19. This was revised in 1993 and from Spring 1995 all ASW training programmes have needed to assess specific competences. Prior to this, the responsibility for assessing the competence of ASWs was left exclusively with local authorities. They still retain a responsibility as seen in section 114 above, but the development of the new courses has probably led to more consistency across authorities in terms of standards.

CCETSW's role has now been taken over by the GSCC (General Social Care Council). The current ASW training programmes in South London, the South West of England, Dorset and Hampshire have been approved by GSCC as conforming to revised regulations now set out in *Assuring Quality for Mental Health Social Work*. The four programmes have adopted common assessment methods and have been validated by Bournemouth University to award 60 credits at third-year honours degree level. Social workers who successfully complete these programmes will have demonstrated that they meet the required ASW competences and are therefore eligible to be considered for approval by the employing agencies. Previously trained ASWs may also have the opportunity to gain these credits by producing a portfolio for assessment. ASWs may then go on to produce further assessed work for a BA (Hons) degree. Completion of these modules leads to the GSCC post-qualifying award in social work (PQSW).

The role of the ASW and their supervision and management needs

DHSS Circular Number LAC(86)15 states:

14. *Approved social workers should have a wider role than reacting to requests for admission to hospital, making the necessary arrangements and ensuring compliance with the law. They should have the specialist knowledge and skills to make appropriate decisions in respect of both clients and their relatives and to gain the confidence of colleagues in the health services with whom they are required to collaborate. They must be familiar with the day-to-day working of an integrated mental health service and be able to assess what other services may be required and know how to mobilise them. They should have access to, consultation with and supervision from qualified and experienced senior officers. Their role is to prevent*

*the necessity for compulsory admission to hospital as well as to make application
where they decide this is appropriate.*

Section 115 and Para. 2.11 of the Code of Practice require the ASW to have some form of
identification. Ideally, this should be a sealed ID card and include: photograph, name, LA details
and contact number, date of appointment as ASW and/or expiry date, signature of director.
Some authorities find it helpful to quote section 115 rights of access on the reverse.

Approved social workers' tasks (with section references)

(* tasks marked with an asterisk can only be performed within the local authority by an ASW)

ss6 and 137	If an application is made, the ASW has the powers of a constable to convey the patient to hospital (see Chapter 11 of Code of Practice).
s8	An ASW may be asked to carry out the functions of guardian by the Local Authority.
*s11(3)	Take such steps as are practicable to inform the nearest relative that an application for admission for assessment has been, or is about to be, made and inform them of their powers of discharge under section 23. This should include reference to s25 RMO blocking power re: danger.
*s11(4)	For an application for admission for treatment or for guardianship, to ensure the nearest relative does not object to an application being made.
*s13(1)	It shall be the duty of an approved social worker to make an application for admission to hospital or a guardianship application in respect of a patient within the area of the local social services authority by which that officer is appointed in any case where he is satisfied that such an application ought to be made and is of the opinion, having regard to any wishes expressed by relatives of the patient or any other relevant circumstances, that it is necessary or proper for the application to be made by him. In carrying out this task the ASW must interview the patient in a 'suitable manner'; consider 'all the circumstances of the case', including past history of the patient's mental disorder, the patient's present condition, the effect on this of any social, family and personal factors, the wishes of the patient, medical opinion. The ASW should consider: informal admission, day-care, out-patient treatment, Community Psychiatric Nursing support, crisis intervention centres, primary health care support, social services provision, friends, relatives, voluntary agencies. The ASW must then decide whether 'detention in a hospital is in all the circumstances of the case the most appropriate way of providing the care and medical treatment of which the patient stands in need' (s13(2)). Although it is important to stress that the ASW is acting as an officer of the local authority who is accountable for the ASW's actions, it should be noted that the ASW also carries a personal responsibility in making this decision.
s13(4)	If required to do so by the nearest relative, the Social Services Department must direct an ASW to assess whether to make an application for detention.
*s13(4)	If the ASW does not apply they must give reasons in writing to the nearest relative.
s14	If the nearest relative applies for section 2 or 3 a social worker must 'interview the patient and produce a report on his social circumstances' for the hospital managers.

*s25B	Where appropriate and having regard to the patient's history, provide a written recommendation in the prescribed form for supervised aftercare.
*s29	In certain circumstances, to apply to the County Court for the displacement and/or appointment of a nearest relative for the patient.
*s115	To enter and inspect premises where there is reasonable cause to believe that patient is not under proper care.
*s135	To apply for a warrant to search for and remove to a place of safety patients or persons living alone or in need of care.
*s136	To interview a person arrested by the Police under s136.

s48 of N.A. Act 1948	
	If a patient is admitted to hospital or Part III (of the National Assistance Act 1948) accommodation, then the local authority must ensure that any moveable property of the patient is protected.

Policy requirements from the Code of Practice

There are a number of points in the Code of Practice where social services departments are required to have a policy. Those managing ASWs may find the following exercise helpful. The list identifies the topic and paragraph number of references in the Code to the need for some sort of policy. Note that section 7 of the Local Authority Social Services Act 1970 as reinforced by *R* v *Islington LBC Ex p Rixon* (1998) requires social services employees to follow such guidance.

Tick if there is already a policy and note the date it was last amended (if available)

Para.	Topic	Policy? *tick/date*	Comments on existing policy or key points if new policy required
1.4	**Interpreters** Guidance; available pool	....	....
1.13	**Ethnicity records** of those admitted under the Act	....	....
2.18	**Nearest Relative displacement s29** Procedures, guidance, assistance	....	....
2.38	**Nearest Relative referrals s13(4)** What amounts to s13(4); response to repeated referrals	....	....
8.1	**Doctor's holding power s5(2)** Performance standards for quick response to referrals	....	....
10.1	**Police powers/place of safety s136** Clear policy needed	....	....
10.19	**Powers of entry s135** Guidance to ASWs on its use	....	....
11.2	**Conveyance of patients** Joint policy with ambulance and police	....	....

Para.	Topic	Policy? *tick/date*	Comments on existing policy or key points if new policy required
13.7	**Guardianship s7 or s37** Detailed guidance needed on eight areas	....	....
21.5	**AWOL s18** Policy needed in case someone in guardianship goes AWOL	....	....
26.3	**Children visiting detained patients** Help hospitals to draw up written policies	....	....
27.4	**CPA** Ensure all staff are familiar with CPA and local arrangements	....	....
28.6	**After-care under supervision s25A** Local liaison arrangements and protocol needed (+ see Annex to Code Supplement)	....	....

Activity **4.1**

Sample questions on the role of the ASW

1a What are the main aspects of law concerned with the appointment of ASWs?

1b What legal protection does an ASW have in carrying out duties under the Mental Health Act 1983?

1c Identify a couple of possible dilemmas for an ASW working in a Home Treatment Team.

2a What are the main responsibilities of an ASW, in terms of interviewing and assessing a patient in their area with a view to a possible section 3 admission?

*2b Take any **one** of these responsibilities and identify potential difficulties for an ASW.*

Chapter 5
Patients concerned in criminal proceedings

Periods of detention, consent to treatment and access to MHR Tribunals for patients covered by Part III of the Mental Health Act 1983

Section Number and purpose	Maximum duration	Can patient apply to MHRT?	Can nearest relative apply to MHRT?	Will there be an automatic MHRT hearing?	*Do consent to treatment rules apply?
35 Remand to hospital for psychiatric report	**28 Days** May be renewed by court for further 28 days to max. 12 weeks	No	No	No	No
36 Remand to hospital for psychiatric treatment	**28 Days** May be renewed by court for further 28 days to max. 12 weeks	No	No	No	Yes
37 Guardianship order by court	**6 months** May be renewed for 6 months and then yearly	Within first 6 months and then in each period	Within first year and then yearly	No	No
37 Hospital order by court	**6 months** May be renewed for 6 months and then yearly	In second 6 months and then in each period	In second 6 months and then in each period	If one has not been held, the Hospital Managers refer to MHRT every 3 years	Yes
37/41 Restriction order by court	**Variable**	In second 6 months and then yearly	There is no nearest relative	If one has not been held, Home Secretary refers every 3 years	Yes

Section Number and purpose	Maximum duration	Can patient apply to MHRT?	Can nearest relative apply to MHRT?	Will there be an automatic MHRT hearing?	*Do consent to treatment rules apply?
38 Interim hospital order by court	12 weeks May be renewed by 28 days at a time to max. 1 year	No	No	No	Yes
45A Hospital and limited directions	**Without limit of time**	In first 6 months, second 6 months and then yearly	No	If one has not been held, the Home Secretary refers to MHRT every 3 years	Yes
46 Transfer to hospital of persons in custody during HM's Pleasure	**Without limit of time**	Within first 6 months and then in each period	No	If one has not been held, the Home Secretary refers to MHRT every 3 years	Yes
47 Transfer to a hospital of a person serving prison sentence	**6 months** May be renewed for 6 months and then yearly	Within first 6 months and then in each period	No	If one has not been held, the Hospital Managers refer to MHRT every 3 years	Yes
47/49 Transfer from prison + restrictions	Restriction order expires on earliest prison release date	In second 6 months period after transfer and then yearly	There is no nearest relative	If one has not been held, the Home Secretary refers to MHRT every 3 years	Yes
48 Transfer to hospital of other prisoners	**Variable**	Within first 6 months and then in each period	No	If one not has been held, the Home Secretary refers to MHRT every 3 years	Yes
48/49 Transfer from prison and restrictions	Restriction order expires on the earliest date of release from prison	In second 6 months period after transfer and then yearly	There is no nearest relative	If one has not been held, the Home Secretary refers to MHRT every 3 years	Yes
136 Police power in public places	**72 hours** Not renewable	No	No	No	No

* Where consent to treatment rules do not apply, a patient is in same position as informal patient and should not be treated without their consent except in an emergency under common law. Chapter 6 has fuller information on consent to treatment.

  – under section 67 the Secretary of State for Health can refer s37 patients to the MHRT at any time

  – under section 71 the Home Secretary can refer restricted patients to the MHRT at any time

  – conditionally discharged restricted patients may apply to MHRT after 1 year and then every 2 years but if the patient is recalled to hospital the Home Secretary must refer to MHRT within one month

Patients involved with the police and the courts

Introduction

Part III of the Mental Health Act 1983 deals with those situations where people can be detained in hospital or received into guardianship as a result of a court order. Similarly, it covers situations where the Home Secretary can direct people to be transferred from penal institutions into hospital. There are significant changes from the position under the 1959 Act. Several of these give effect to recommendations which were made in the Butler Report of 1975 (Cmnd 6244). One of the report's main conclusions was that too many mentally abnormal offenders were being inappropriately placed in prison. Sections 35, 36 and 38 of the 1983 Act were all new attempts to tackle this problem. There was a delay in their implementation until 1984 when it was believed resources would be in place to cope with these new patients. The table at the start of this chapter provides a summary of the main sections noting their purpose, duration, whether there is access to Mental Health Review Tribunals and whether consent to treatment provisions apply. Section 136 is included because it is sometimes used with offenders. There is further legislation, apart from the Mental Health Act, which affects patients who offend. This is included here in a summary of law which is relevant at different points in an offender's career:

(1)   at the time of police involvement

(2)   before the trial

(3)   at the trial (where mental disorder may be used as a defence)

(4)   at sentencing

(5)   after sentencing.

This approach mirrors that taken by Brenda Hoggett in *Mental Health Law* (1996).

(1) Police powers

(i) Detention under section 136
The wording of this section is straightforward:

> *136(1) If a constable finds in a place to which the public has access a person who appears to him to be suffering from mental disorder and to be in immediate need of care or control, the constable may, if he thinks it necessary to do so in the interests of that person or for the protection of other persons, remove that person to a place of safety within the meaning of section 135. (2) A person removed to a place of safety under this section may be detained there for a period not exceeding 72 hours for the purpose of enabling him to be examined by a registered medical practitioner and to be interviewed by an ASW and of making any necessary arrangements for his treatment or care.*

The officer does not have to suspect that any criminal offence has been committed.

This has proved to be a somewhat contentious piece of legislation, especially in London. MIND has undertaken some detailed research on its operation (see booklist) and one conclusion was that the power was used disproportionately with black people. The Code of Practice (para. 10.4a) states that its use with people from ethnic minorities should be monitored. Patients arrested under section 136 have the right to have another person of their choice informed of the arrest and of their whereabouts. If a police station is used as the place of safety, they have a right of access to legal advice. If somewhere else is used, the Code (para. 10.9) recommends access to legal advice if it is requested. Section 136(2) makes it clear that an assessment should be carried out by both an ASW and a doctor. If the doctor arrives first and concludes admission to hospital is unnecessary or the person agrees to informal admission, the individual should still be seen by an ASW. Only if the doctor concludes that the person is not mentally disordered at all should they be released before the arrival of the ASW (para. 10.8a). Many areas still use police stations as places of safety but the 1999 edition of the Code (para. 10.5) recommends:

> *as a general rule it is preferable for a person thought to be suffering from mental disorder to be detained in a hospital rather than a Police Station.*

(ii) Diversion, interrogation and prosecution

Apart from section 136 the police have a number of options to choose from when they are dealing with a possible offender whom they think might be mentally disordered: check if the person is an absconding detained patient and then return them to the hospital under sections 18 or 138; persuade the person to co-operate while they set up an informal or compulsory admission; use their statutory powers of arrest. Under the Police and Criminal Evidence Act 1984 (PACE) there is a Code of Practice which covers the detention, treatment and questioning of persons by police officers. This will apply where the officer suspects, or is told in good faith, that a person may be mentally ill or have significant learning difficulties or be unable to understand the significance of questions or, indeed, the significance of their own answers. If the person is detained, an 'appropriate adult' must be informed and asked to come to the police station. A person who is trained or experienced in dealing with mentally disordered people may often be seen as more appropriate than an unqualified relative. The appropriate adult should be present when the individual is told of their rights or can have them read again. They can also require the presence of a lawyer. Unless delay would involve serious risk to person or property, a mentally disordered person should not be interviewed or asked to sign a statement until the appropriate adult is present. The appropriate adult is not just an observer. They have a role in advising the person being interviewed, observing the fairness of the interview and of facilitating communication with the interviewee. If a decision is taken to prosecute, the case is passed to the Crown Prosecution Service. Among other factors, they will consider the likely effect of prosecution on people who are young, old, infirm or mentally ill. In the case of mental illness, the Crown Prosecutor will require independent evidence of the illness and the likely adverse effects of prosecution.

(iii) Other relevant police powers

By section 17 of the PACE Act 1984, a constable may enter and search any premises to execute a warrant; to arrest a person for an arrestable offence; to recapture someone unlawfully at large whom is he pursuing; or to save life or limb or to prevent serious damage to property. There are limited circumstances in which a common law power of arrest may be made. In *Bibby v Chief Constable of Essex Police* (Court of Appeal 2000) these circumstances were summarised: a sufficiently real and present threat to the peace; the threat coming from the person to be arrested; conduct clearly interfering with the rights of others with its natural consequence being 'not wholly unreasonable violence' from a third party; and unreasonable conduct from the person to be arrested.

(2) Procedure before trial

There is a presumption in favour of remanding a person on bail rather than in custody. This could even include a condition of residence at a hospital while, for example, reports are prepared. In these circumstances, however, the patient would be informal and not subject to detention. Where a person might otherwise be remanded to prison, the Mental Health Act 1983 introduced two new powers:

(i) Section 35. Remand to hospital for report on accused's mental condition
Subsection (3) allows an order to be made if:

> *(a) the Court is satisfied, on the written or oral evidence of a registered medical practitioner, that there is reason to suspect that the accused person is suffering from mental illness, psychopathic disorder, severe mental impairment or mental impairment; and (b) the Court is of the opinion that it would be impracticable for a report on his mental condition to be made if he were remanded on bail.*

There must also be evidence that a hospital bed would be available within seven days, beginning with the date of the remand. While waiting for a bed, the accused must be kept in a 'place of safety', which for the purposes of this section could be: 'any police station, prison, or remand centre, or any hospital the managers of which are willing temporarily to receive him' (s55(1)). The remand is for a maximum 28 days although the court may renew this for further periods of 28 days to a maximum of 12 weeks. Part IV provisions on consent to treatment do not apply so the person should not be treated without their consent except in an emergency under common law. To overcome this, some psychiatrists have sought a section 3 detention to run alongside the section 35. Section 5 does not specifically rule this out and the Code of Practice states that it might be considered if there is a delay in getting to court. The use of section 36 might be more appropriate in most such cases.

(ii) Section 36. Remand of accused person to hospital for treatment
This may only be used by the Crown Court and is restricted to those cases where it would be an alternative to a remand in custody. It applies to people waiting for trial or sentence and requires the written or oral evidence of two doctors that the person is 'suffering from mental illness or severe mental impairment of a nature or degree which makes it appropriate for him to be detained in a hospital for treatment'. The remand is for a maximum of 28 days although the court may renew this for further periods of 28 days to a maximum of 12 weeks. Part IV provisions on consent to treatment apply. Again there must be evidence that a hospital bed would be available within seven days, beginning with the date of the remand. While waiting for a bed, the accused must be kept in a 'place of safety' which, for the purposes of this section could be: 'any police station, prison or remand centre, or any hospital the managers of which are willing temporarily to receive him' (s 55(1)). It is possible that someone may have to wait for more than three months to appear in the Crown Court. In these circumstances, the general powers of the Secretary of State to transfer prisoners may apply.

Section 48. Removal to hospital of other prisoners
This section gives the Home Secretary powers to direct the transfer to hospital of a person who is waiting for trial or sentence, and who has been remanded in custody. The section applies to people who are: detained under the Immigration Act 1971; civil prisoners; remanded in custody by a magistrates' court; or otherwise detained in a prison or remand centre but not serving a custodial sentence. The Home Secretary needs two medical reports stating that the 'person is suffering from mental illness or severe mental impairment of a nature or degree which makes it

appropriate for him to be detained in a hospital for medical treatment and that he is in urgent need of such treatment'. Periods of detention in hospital may vary but a civil or Immigration Act prisoner can never be detained longer than they would have been in prison. Part IV provisions on consent to treatment apply.

(iv) Unfit to plead (Criminal Procedure (Insanity and Unfitness to Plead) Act 1991)
Where an accused person is unfit to be tried, there is provision for a 'trial of the facts' to determine whether the jury is satisfied beyond reasonable doubt that the accused did the act or made the omission charged against him. Home Office Circular No. 93/1991 sets out guidance on the trial of the facts and summarises the disposal options which include: a hospital admission order, guardianship order, supervision and treatment order, absolute discharge.

(3) Mental disorder as a defence

(i) The insanity defence where sentences are fixed by law (i.e. murder)
The accused was 'labouring under such defect of reason from disease of the mind as to not know the nature and quality of the act he was doing, or, if he did know it, that he did not know it was wrong' (the M'Naghten Rules). If the defence is used successfully, the judge must make the equivalent of a hospital order with restrictions on discharge. Its use is rare. This is still a requirement following the changes of the Criminal Procedure (Insanity and Unfitness to Plead) Act 1991.

(ii) Diminished responsibility. Section 2 of the Homicide Act 1957
The accused was suffering from such abnormality of mind as to substantially impair mental responsibility for the killing. If successful, the judge has discretion in sentencing. Conviction will be for manslaughter, not murder, so there is no mandatory life sentence.

(iii) Infanticide Act 1938
May apply to a woman who kills a child under one year of age if her mind 'is disturbed by reason of not having fully recovered from the effect of giving birth to the child or by reason of the effect of lactation consequent on the birth'. The court may impose any appropriate sentence.

(4) Sentencing

There are five possible orders which involve a psychiatric element.

(i) Hospital or Guardianship Order. Section 37 of the Mental Health Act 1983
This may be made by the Crown Court in cases where an offender is convicted. A magistrates' court may make an order, even without a conviction, as long as they are satisfied that the offender committed the act or made the omission in question. Requirements set out in section 37(2) are that:

   (a) *the Court is satisfied, on the written or oral evidence of two registered medical practitioners, that the offender is suffering from mental illness, psychopathic disorder, severe mental impairment or mental impairment and that either –*

     (i) *the mental disorder from which the offender is suffering is of a nature or degree which makes it appropriate for him to be detained in a hospital for medical treatment and, in the case of psychopathic disorder or mental impairment, that such treatment is likely to alleviate or prevent a deterioration of his condition; or*

> (ii) *in the case of an offender who has attained the age of 16 years, the mental disorder is of a nature or degree which warrants his reception into guardianship under this Act; and*

> (b) *the Court is of the opinion, having regard to all the circumstances including the nature of the offence and the character and antecedents of the offender, and to the other available methods of dealing with him, that the most suitable method of disposing of the case is by means of an order under this section.*

The order is for up to six months in the first instance. This may be renewed for a further six months and then for a year at a time. Apart from a delay until after 6 months for an appeal to the MHRT (there is a route for an appeal through the court system within this period).

For a hospital order the effect is as if the person were subject to section 3. Part IV applies (see Chapter 6). There must also be evidence that a hospital bed would be available within 28 days, beginning with the date of the order. While waiting for a bed a patient may be kept in a 'place of safety', which for the purposes of this section could be: 'any police station, prison or remand centre, or any hospital the managers of which are willing temporarily to receive him' (s55(1)).

Guardianship orders are rare. The order can only be made if the proposed guardian agrees to it. If the patient absconds from the place they are required to live, they may be recaptured and returned there. Otherwise, there are no effective sanctions for a patient refusing to co-operate. The Butler Report considered that collaboration between relevant agencies might lead to a welcome increase in the use of guardianship.

(ii) Interim Hospital Order. Section 38 of the Mental Health Act 1983
If a court is uncertain if a full hospital order is appropriate, they can test this out by making an interim order. The order can be made for up to 12 weeks at first instance and can then be renewed by the court for periods of up to 28 days at a time, to a maximum of one year. In effect, the court is reserving final judgement. Part IV applies.

(iii) Restriction Order. Sections 37/41 of the Mental Health Act 1983
The court must have the same evidence needed to make a hospital order and one of the doctors must attend to give evidence in person. Section 41 (1) states:

> *Where a hospital order is made in respect of an offender by the Crown Court, and it appears to the court, having regard to the nature of the offence, the antecedents of the offender and the risk of his committing further offences if set at large, that it is necessary for the protection of the public from serious harm so to do, the court may, subject to the provisions of this section, further order that the offender shall be subject to the special restrictions set out in this section, either without limit of time or during such period as may be specified in the order; and an order under this section shall be known as a 'restriction order'.*

The main restrictions are that the patient can only be discharged, given leave of absence or transferred to another hospital with the approval of the Home Secretary. The Home Secretary may discharge the patient absolutely or conditionally. For the latter, the patient is subject to compulsory after-care which will involve supervision by either a probation officer or social worker. The order may be without limit of time, in which case there is no renewal process and the only review of the order would be via the MHRT process. Sometimes, the restrictions are placed on the person for a fixed period of time (e.g. two years), after which the order is treated as a hospital order without restrictions.

(iv) Hospital and limitation directions. Section 45A of the Mental Health Act 1983
This provision was brought in by the Crime (Sentences) Act 1997 on 1 October 1997. It is referred to as the 'Hybrid Order' as it is a prison sentence accompanied by hospital and limitation directions. It is only available to the Crown Court. Grounds are that the person is suffering from psychopathic disorder (this may be extended to other mental disorders in the future). Written or oral evidence from two doctors is required and the treatability test applies.

(v) Psychiatric probation orders
Probation orders can be made in any court and for any offence other than one with a fixed penalty but they do require a conviction. The offender is then supervised by a probation officer for a specified period between six months and three years. The court must have evidence from a doctor approved under the Mental Health Act 1983. The doctor must state that the person's mental condition requires, and may be susceptible to, treatment but that the person does not need to be subject to a hospital order. The court may then specify where treatment should take place: as an in-patient in a hospital or mental nursing home; as an out-patient at a specified hospital or place; by or under the direction of a named doctor. The court must explain all the requirements of the order to the offender and obtain their consent to the order. If, subsequently, the person refuses to co-operate with one of the conditions, the doctor can only report this to the supervising officer who may take proceedings for breach of protection.

(5) After sentencing

(i) Transfers from prison. Section 47 of the Mental Health Act 1983
It is still possible for a prisoner to be transferred to a psychiatric hospital even after sentencing. The Home Secretary can order their transfer under section 47 if satisfied by reports from at least two doctors:

(a) *that the said person is suffering from mental illness, psychopathic disorder, severe mental impairment or mental impairment; and*

(b) *that the mental disorder from which that person is suffering is of a nature or degree which makes it appropriate for him to be detained in a hospital for medical treatment and, in the case of psychopathic disorder or mental impairment, that such treatment is likely to alleviate or prevent a deterioration of his condition.*

The transfer direction has the same effect as a section 37 hospital order made without restrictions and the patient is subject to consent to treatment provisions. Commonly, a restriction direction is also made under section 49. This has the same effect as a restriction order under section 41 described above. If the offender was sentenced to a fixed term of imprisonment, the restriction lifts on the expiry of the sentence (allowing for remission).

(ii) Transfer of persons kept in custody during Her Majesty's pleasure. Section 46 MHAct 1983
This covers members of the Armed Forces detained 'during Her Majesty's pleasure' (indefinitely). The Home Secretary may direct them to be detained in a hospital. The direction has the same effect as a hospital order with restrictions with no limit of time.

The flowchart in Figure 5.1 (p. 77) shows potential routes for someone who is arrested by the police for an offence or under section 136. The various elements of the law referred to can then be checked against the summaries in this chapter.

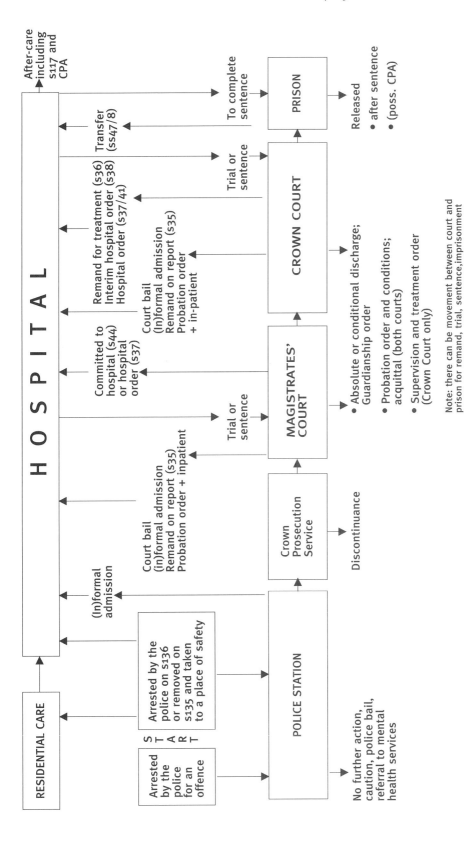

Figure 5.1 The police, the courts and mental health

Extracts from Basant K Puri, Robert A Brown, Heather J Mckee and Ian H Treasaden, *Mental Health Law: A Practical Guide* (Hodder Education, 2005).
© 2005 Basant K Puri, Robert A Brown, Heather J Mckee and Ian H Treasaden. Reproduced by permission of Hodder & Stoughton.

The role of the appropriate adult

This section contains extracts of the Police and Criminal Evidence Act 1984 Codes of Practice (2004). (Relevant Home Office Circulars not covered here include 66/1990 and 12/1995.)

C1.7(b) In the case of a person who is mentally disordered or mentally vulnerable, 'the appropriate adult' means:

- *a relative, guardian or other person responsible for their care or custody;*
- *someone experienced in dealing with mentally disordered or mentally vulnerable people but who is not a police officer or employed by the police;*
- *failing these, some other responsible adult aged 18 or over who is not a police officer or employed by the police.*

Note 1D. *In the case of people who are mentally disordered or otherwise mentally vulnerable, it may be more satisfactory if the appropriate adult is someone experienced or trained in their care rather than a relative lacking such qualifications. But if the detainee prefers a relative to a better qualified stranger or objects to a particular person, their wishes should, if practicable, be respected.*

C11.17 If an appropriate adult is present at an interview, they shall be informed:

- *they are not expected to act simply as an observer; and*
- *the purpose of their presence is, to:*
  - *advise the person being interviewed;*
  - *observe whether the interview is being conducted properly and fairly;*
  - *facilitate communication with the person being interviewed.*

[The appropriate adult's role is not just in the interview, e.g. Annex A 5 to Code C: An intimate search ... of a mentally disordered or otherwise mentally vulnerable person may take place only in the presence of an appropriate adult of the same sex, unless the detainee specifically requests a particular adult of the opposite sex who is readily available.]

C1.4 If an Officer has any suspicion, or is told in good faith, that a person of any age may be mentally disordered or otherwise mentally vulnerable, in the absence of clear evidence to dispel that suspicion, the person shall be treated as such for the purposes of this Code.

Note 1G. *'Mentally vulnerable' applies to any detainee who, because of their mental state or capacity, may not understand the significance of what is said, of questions, or of their replies. Links the term mental disorder to section 1 of the Mental Health Act but also states that if the Custody Officer has any doubts about the mental state/ capacity of a person an AA should be called.*

Note 1E. *A person should always be given an opportunity to consult a solicitor privately without the AA being present.*

Note 1F. *A solicitor or independent custody visitor may not act as appropriate adult.*

Note 1I. *Custody officer should remind the AA and detained person of the right to legal advice and record any reason for waiving this.*

Code C: Annex E – Summary of provisions relating to mentally disordered and otherwise mentally vulnerable people (August 2004 edition)

1. *If an officer has any suspicion, or is told in good faith, that a person of any age may be mentally disordered or otherwise mentally vulnerable, or mentally incapable of understanding the significance of questions or their replies, that person shall be treated as mentally disordered or otherwise mentally vulnerable for the purposes of this Code. See paragraph 1.4**

2. *In the case of a person who is mentally disordered or otherwise mentally vulnerable, 'the appropriate adult' means:*
   a) *a relative, guardian or other person responsible for their care or custody;*
   b) *someone experienced in dealing with mentally disordered or mentally vulnerable people but who is not a police officer or employed by the police;*
   c) *failing these, some other responsible adult aged 18 or over who is not a police officer or employed by the police.*
   See paragraph 1.7(b) and Note 1D

3. *If the custody officer authorises the detention of a person who is mentally vulnerable or appears to be suffering from a mental disorder, the custody officer must, as soon as practicable, inform the appropriate adult of the grounds for detention and the person's whereabouts, and ask the adult to come to the police station to see them. If the appropriate adult:*
   - *is already at the station when information is given as in paragraphs 3.1 to 3.5*, the information must be given in their presence.*
   - *Is not at the station when the provisions of paragraph 3.1 to 3.5* are complied with, these provisions must be complied with again in their presence once they arrive.*
   See paragraphs 3.15 to 3.17*

4. *If the appropriate adult, having been informed of the right to legal advice, considers legal advice should be taken, the provisions of section 6 apply as if the mentally disordered or otherwise mentally vulnerable person had requested access to legal advice. See paragraph 3.19 and Note E1**

5. *The custody officer must make sure a person receives appropriate clinical attention as soon as reasonably practicable if the person appears to be suffering from a mental disorder or in urgent cases immediately call the nearest health care professional or an ambulance. It is not intended these provisions delay the transfer of a detainee to a place of safety under the Mental Health Act 1983, section 136 if that is applicable. If an assessment under that Act is to take place at a police station, the custody officer must consider whether an appropriate health care professional should be called to conduct an initial clinical check on the detainee. See paragraph 9.5 and 9.6**

6. *It is imperative a mentally disordered or otherwise mentally vulnerable person detained under the Mental Health Act 1983, section 136 be assessed as soon as possible. If that assessment is to take place at the police station, an approved social worker and registered medical practitioner shall be called to the station as*

soon as possible in order to interview and examine the detainee. Once the detainee has been interviewed, examined and suitable arrangements been made for their treatment or care, they can no longer be detained under section 136. A detainee should be immediately discharged from detention if a registered medical practitioner having examined them, concludes they are not mentally disordered within the meaning of the Act. See paragraph 3.16*

7. *If a mentally disordered or otherwise mentally vulnerable person is cautioned in the absence of the appropriate adult, the caution must be repeated in the appropriate adult's presence. See paragraph 10.12**

8. *A mentally disordered or otherwise mentally vulnerable person must not be interviewed or asked to provide or sign a written statement in the absence of the appropriate adult unless the provisions of paragraphs 11.1 or 11.18 to 11.20* apply. Questioning in these circumstances may not continue in the absence of the appropriate adult once sufficient information to avert the risk has been obtained. A record shall be made of the grounds for any decision to begin an interview in these circumstances. See paragraphs 11.1, 11.5 and 11.18 to 11.20**

9. *If the appropriate adult is present at an interview, they shall be informed they are not expected to act simply as an observer and the purposes of their presence are to:*
   - *advise the interviewee*
   - *observe whether or not the interview is being conducted properly and fairly*
   - *facilitate communication with the interviewee.*

See paragraph 11.17*

10. *If the detention of a mentally disordered or otherwise mentally vulnerable person is reviewed by a review officer or a superintendent, the appropriate adult must, if available at the time, be given an opportunity to make representations to the officer about the need for continuing detention. See paragraph 15.3**

11. *If the custody officer charges a mentally disordered or otherwise mentally vulnerable person with an offence or takes such other action as is appropriate when there is sufficient evidence for a prosecution this must be done in the presence of the appropriate adult. The written notice embodying any charge must be given to the appropriate adult. See paragraphs 16.1 to 16.4A**

12. *An intimate or strip search of a mentally disordered or otherwise mentally vulnerable person may take place only in the presence of the appropriate adult of the same sex, unless the detainee specifically requests the presence of a particular adult of the opposite sex. A strip search may take place in the absence of an appropriate adult only in cases of urgency when there is a risk of serious harm to the detainee or others. See Annex A, paragraphs 5 and 11(c)**

13. *Particular care must be taken when deciding whether to use any form of approved restraints on a mentally disordered or otherwise mentally vulnerable person in a locked cell. See paragraph 8/2**

Notes for guidance

E1 *The purpose of the provision at paragraph 3.19* is to protect the rights of a mentally disordered or otherwise mentally vulnerable detained person who does not understand the significance of what is said to them. If the detained person* wants to exercise the right to legal advice, the appropriate action should be taken and not delayed until the appropriate adult arrives. A mentally disordered or otherwise mentally vulnerable detained person should always be given an opportunity, when an appropriate adult is called to the police station, to consult privately with a solicitor in the absence of the appropriate adult if they want.

E2 Although people who are mentally disordered or otherwise mentally vulnerable are often capable of providing reliable evidence, they may, without knowing or wanting to do so, be particularly prone in certain circumstances to proved information that may be unreliable, misleading or self-incriminating. Special care should always be taken when questioning such a person, and the appropriate adult should be involved if there is any doubt about a person's mental state or capacity. Because of the risk of unreliable evidence, it is important to obtain corroboration of any facts admitted whenever possible.

E3 Because of the risks referred to in Note E2, which the presence of the appropriate adult is intended to minimise, officers of superintendent rank or above should exercise their discretion to authorise the commencement of an interview in the appropriate adult's absence only in exceptional cases, if it is necessary to avert an immediate risk of serious harm. See paragraphs 11.1, 11.18 to 11.20*

* *Paragraph references are to the Codes of Practice – Code C Detention, treatment and questioning of persons by police officers.*

Activity 5.1

Sample questions on patients involved in criminal proceedings

1a What grounds need to exist before a person can be placed on a Section 37 Hospital Order under the Mental Health Act 1983?

1b In what circumstances might restrictions be put on such an order and what are the main likely effects of such restrictions?

1c What aspects of the Mental Health Act might lead an ASW to become involved with such a patient?

2a A woman is arrested by the police and is brought to the police station. The police suspect that she may be suffering from a mental disorder. Give two reasons why an ASW might be called to the station.

2b List some of the issues about using a police station to hold someone who might be mentally ill? How could an ASW ameliorate any problems?

Chapter 6
Consent to treatment and mental capacity

Consent to treatment under the Mental Health Act 1983

Introduction

The purpose of Part IV of the Act is to clarify the circumstances in which treatment for mental disorder may be given without the consent of a detained patient. This was often a contentious issue under the 1959 Mental Health Act, which gave no specific guidance on treatment. Although the 1983 Act introduced a fairly clear set of rules to follow, these have, in turn, become somewhat contentious and a number of complications have arisen from case law.

The main principle adopted by the Act is that there are some patients who are liable to be detained who may need to be given treatment without their consent. Further, this may be seen as reasonable given the fact of their detention. Certain procedures, however, should be followed in order to offer safeguards. These essentially involve a second medical opinion from outside the hospital for more serious forms of treatment in those cases where valid consent cannot be obtained from the patient. This absence of consent could be the result either of the patient objecting to the treatment, or of their being unable to give valid consent (e.g. because of mental incapacity). For the most serious treatments (such as psychosurgery), a second opinion and the consent of the patient are required. Because of the invasive nature of these treatments, the safeguards are also extended to informal patients. The Mental Health Act Commission has a general duty to oversee the operation of this part of the Act.

Patients not covered by Part IV of the Act are in the same position as any other patients in a general hospital and cannot be treated without their consent except where common law would allow it (e.g. in an emergency). It is particularly important to understand not just what the procedures are, but which patients are covered by them, as not all detained patients are included. Generally, those patients liable to detention for periods of more than 72 hours are covered, with the exception of people remanded for reports by the courts under section 35. Details of which sections are covered by the rules are included in full in the checklist and flowchart (Figure 6.1) later in this chapter. The grids which can be found in this *Guide* at the start of Chapter 2 (for patients detained under Part II) and at the start of Chapter 5 (for patients involved in criminal proceedings) also provide a quick visual guide as to which patients are covered by the Part IV rules and which are not.

A definition of consent

Paragraph 15.13 of the Code of Practice states:

'Consent' is the voluntary and continuing permission of the patient to receive a particular treatment, based on an adequate knowledge of the purpose, nature, likely effects and risks of that treatment including the likelihood of its success and any alternatives to it. Permission given under any unfair or undue pressure is not 'consent'.

Common law position for most patients

Unless Part IV of the Act specifically covers a situation, the common law will apply. This requires the valid consent of the patient to proposed medical treatment except in certain circumstances. These are discussed in paragraphs 15.18 to 15.24 of the Code of Practice. In particular, para. 15.21 states:

There are particular considerations that doctors must take into account in discharging their duty of care for those who lack capacity to consent. Treatment for their condition may be prescribed for them in their best interests under the common law doctrine of necessity. According to the decision in the case of Re F.*, if treatment is given 'in the patient's best interests', to a patient who is not capable of giving consent, the treatment must be:*

- *necessary to save life or prevent a deterioration or ensure an improvement in the patient's physical or mental health; and*
- *in accordance with a practice accepted at the time by a reasonable body of medical opinion skilled in the particular form of treatment in question.*

Note that this does not restrict intervention to emergency situations.

Capacity: the basic principles

The Code of Practice states at paras 15.10 and 15.11 that an individual:

is presumed to have the capacity to make a treatment decision unless he or she:

- *is unable to take in and retain the information material to the decision especially as to the likely consequences of having or not having the treatment; or*
- *is unable to believe the information; or*
- *is unable to weigh the information in the balance as part of a process of arriving at the decision.*

It must be remembered:

- *any assessment as to an individual's capacity has to be made in relation to a particular treatment or admission proposal;*
- *capacity in an individual with a mental disorder can be variable over time and should be assessed at the time the admission or treatment is proposed;*
- *all assessments of an individual's capacity should be fully recorded in the patient's medical notes.*

15.11. Where an individual lacks capacity at a particular time, it may be possible to establish that there was an advance refusal of treatment in the past. To be valid, an advance refusal must be clearly verifiable and must relate to the type of treatment now proposed. If there is any reason to doubt the reliability of an advance refusal of treatment, then an application to the court for a declaration could be made. The individual must have had the capacity to make an advance refusal when it was made. An advanced refusal of medical treatment for mental disorder does not prevent the authorisation of such treatment by Part IV of the Act in the circumstances where those provisions apply.

Mental capacity and advanced refusal

Re C (1994) was a key case concerning consent. C was a Broadmoor patient diagnosed as suffering from paranoid schizophrenia. The court recognised C's capacity to refuse amputation of a gangrenous foot (a condition which was said to be life-threatening). The criteria now set out in the Code of Practice para. 15.10 (above) were used to determine his competence. Thorpe J. was satisfied that C 'has understood and retained the relevant treatment information, that in his own way he believes it, and that in the same fashion he has arrived at a clear choice'. He also accepted that C had made an advanced directive that he never wanted such treatment in the future so that, if he lost capacity, it would still not be possible to operate. This was an important case in recognising the validity of advanced refusals of treatment.

Best interests

For a treatment to be necessary in a patient's best interests, it must be necessary to save life or to alleviate or prevent deterioration in their physical or mental health. In deciding whether treatment is in a patient's best interests, the doctor must act in accordance with a practice accepted at the time by a responsible body of medical opinion skilled in the speciality (i.e. the Bolam principle).

Consent

Many people who are mentally disordered will be able to give or withhold valid consent to particular forms of treatment. Consent needs to be based on an adequate broad knowledge of the proposed treatment, i.e. its nature, purpose, possible benefits and risks and any possible alternatives. The person should understand what is likely to happen if the treatment is not given.

Consent should not be given under duress. It can also be withdrawn at any point. It is generally held that a child under the age of 16 may give consent if they fulfil the requirements of the 'Gillick' test, i.e. that they have reached a level of understanding to appreciate fully what treatment is being proposed, its potential benefits, risks and alternatives.

There have been several controversial decisions (e.g. involving treatment of women who are pregnant by making them have caesarean section deliveries – this has involved treatment under the Mental Health Act as well as under common law) in recent years and this is an area where ASWs and others need to be especially careful to take advice as to the latest legal position.

After the *R* v *Collins* case, guidelines were issued by the Court of Appeal in July 1998. These apply in cases involving capacity when surgical or invasive treatment might be needed by any patient. They also extend, where relevant, to medical practitioners and health professionals generally as well as to hospital authorities. They are set out below.

This is then followed by:

- a checklist covering consent to treatment issues

- a flowchart to help illustrate the procedures involved.

R v *Collins* **case guidelines**

1. The guidelines had no application where a patient was competent to accept or refuse treatment. In principle a patient could remain competent notwithstanding detention under the Mental Health Act 1983.

2. If the patient was competent and refused to consent to the treatment, an application to the High Court for a declaration was pointless. In that situation, the advice given to the patient should be recorded. For their own protection, hospital authorities should seek unequivocal assurances from the patient, to be recorded in writing, that the refusal represented an informed decision. If the patient was unwilling to sign a written indication of refusal, that too should be noted in writing. Such a written indication was merely a record for evidential purposes. It should not be confused with or regarded as a disclaimer.

3. If the patient was incapable of giving or refusing consent, either in the long term or temporarily, the patient had to be cared for according to the authority's judgement of the patient's best interests. Where the patient had given an advance directive, before becoming incapable, treatment and care should normally be subject to the advance directive. However, if there was reason to doubt the reliability of the advance directive, then an application for a declaration could be made.

4. Concern over capacity. The authority should identify as soon as possible where there was concern about a patient's competence to consent to or refuse treatment.

5. If the capacity of the patient was seriously in doubt, it should be assessed as a matter of priority. In many cases the patient's general practitioner, or other responsible doctor, might be sufficiently qualified to make the necessary assessment. But in serious or complex cases involving difficult issues about the future health and well-being or even life of the patient, the issue of capacity should be examined by an independent psychiatrist, ideally one approved under section12(2) of the Mental Health Act 1983. If, following that assessment, there remained a serious doubt about the patient's competence and the seriousness or complexity of the issues in the particular case might require the involvement of the court, the psychiatrist should further consider whether the patient was incapable by reason of mental disorder of managing her property or affairs. If so, that patient might not be able to instruct a solicitor and would require a guardian *ad litem* in any court proceedings. The health authority should seek legal advice as quickly as possible. If a declaration was to be sought the patient's solicitors should be informed immediately and if practicable, they should have a proper opportunity to take instructions and apply for legal aid where necessary. Potential witnesses for the health authority should be made aware of the criteria laid down in *re MB (Caesarean Section)* (*Times*, 18 April 1997; 2 FCR 541) and this case, together with any guidance issued by the Department of Health, and the British Medical Association.

6. If the patient was unable to instruct solicitors, or was believed to be incapable of doing so, the health authority or its legal advisers had to notify the Official Solicitor and invite him to act as guardian *ad litem*. If the Official Solicitor agreed, he would no doubt wish, if possible, to arrange for the patient to be interviewed to ascertain her wishes and to explore reasons for any refusal of treatment. The Official Solicitor could be contacted through the Urgent Court Business Officer out of hours on 020-7936-6000.

7. The hearing before the judge should be *inter partes*. As the order made in her absence would not be binding on the patient unless she was represented either by a guardian *ad litem*, if incapable of giving instructions, or, if capable, by counsel or solicitor, a declaration granted *ex parte* was of no assistance to the health authority. Although the Official Solicitor would not act for a patient if she was capable of instructing a solicitor, the court might, in any event, call on the Official Solicitor, who had considerable expertise in these matters, to assist as an *amicus curiae*.

8. It was axiomatic that the judge was provided with accurate and all relevant information. That should include the reasons for the proposed treatment, the risks involved in the proposed treatment, and in not proceeding with it, whether any alternative treatment existed, and the reasons, if ascertainable, why the patient was refusing the proposed treatment. The judge would need sufficient information to reach an informed conclusion about the patient's capacity and where it arose, the issue of best interests.

9. The precise terms of any order should be recorded and approved by the judge before its terms were transmitted to the health authority. The patient should be accurately informed of the precise terms.

10. Applicants for emergency orders from the High Court made without first issuing and serving the relevant applications and evidence in support had a duty to comply with the procedural requirements ... as soon as possible after the urgency hearing.

Conclusion – there might be occasions when, assuming a serious question arose about the competence of the patient, the situation which faced the Authority might be so urgent and the consequences so desperate that it was impracticable to attempt to comply with the guidelines, which should be approached for what they were – guidelines. Where delay itself might cause serious damage to the patient's health or put the patient's life at risk then formulaic compliance with the guidelines would be inappropriate. [1998] 3 WLR 936.

Checklist on consent to treatment

Go through the steps below to check the provisions in Part IV of the Act. At 'exit' points go to common law position set out on an earlier page.

1 *Does Part IV of the Mental Health Act 1983 apply to the patient? If they are detained under sections 2, 3, 36, 37, 38, 45a, 46, 47 or 48 then the answer is yes. If they are informal, subject only to guardianship (under ss 7 or 37) or detained under sections 4, 5, 35, 135 or 136, the answer is no and you should exit at this point unless the treatment is psychosurgery or sex hormone implants.*

2 *Is the treatment in question given under the direction of the RMO (responsible medical officer) and is it a treatment for mental disorder? If not, exit.*

3 *If the treatment is medication go to (4). If it is ECT, go to (5). If psychosurgery or the surgical implantation of hormones for the purpose of reducing male sex drive, go to (6). If it is none of these (i.e. not listed in the Act or in the regulations), then treatment may be given without the consent of the patient. An example would be nursing care. See section 145 for a definition of treatment.*

4   Have three months elapsed during this period of detention since the medication was first given? If not, treatment may be given without the patient's consent. If, however, three months have elapsed, then go to (5).

5   For ECT (or medication after three months) then either:
(a)   the patient's consent is needed, together with a certificate verifying the validity of this consent (Form 38). This certificate must be completed either by the RMO or by a doctor appointed by the MHAC (Mental Health Act Commission); or, if this is not possible,
(b)   a certificate is needed, completed by a doctor appointed by the MHAC, stating that the treatment is appropriate (Form 39). Before signing, the doctor must consult with a nurse and with one other professional who is concerned with the patient's treatment. The staff who are consulted should make a record of this in the patient's notes.

If neither (a) nor (b) applies, treatment cannot be given except in an emergency when the provisions of section 62 apply. See (7) below.

6   For psychosurgery or surgical implantation of hormones for the purpose of reducing male sex drive, the following are required before treatment can be given to any patient (formal or informal):
(a)   the consent of the patient, and
(b)   a certificate verifying the validity of this consent signed by a doctor and two other people appointed by the MHAC, and
(c)   a certificate that treatment is appropriate signed by a doctor appointed by the MHAC who has consulted a nurse and another professional concerned with the patient's treatment.

If any of (a) to (c) do not apply, then treatment cannot be given except in an emergency when the provisions of section 62 apply. See (7) below.

7   Section 62 states that procedures as in (5) and (6) above do not apply to any treatment which is immediately necessary to save the patient's life; or
(a)   which (not being irreversible) is immediately necessary to prevent a serious deterioration of his condition; or
(c)   which (not being irreversible or hazardous) is immediately necessary to alleviate serious suffering by the patient; or
(d)   which (not being irreversible or hazardous) is immediately necessary and represents the minimum interference necessary to prevent the patient from behaving violently or being a danger to himself or others.

Note: Section 62 only applies to the specific forms of treatment covered under (5) and (6) above and to patients included under Part IV of the Act. They are sometimes confused with the common law position. The MHAC, in para. 7.6 of its Second Biennial Report, stated, in relation to section 62, 'where this section is invoked a request should generally simultaneously be made for a second opinion, so that repeated use does not arise'.

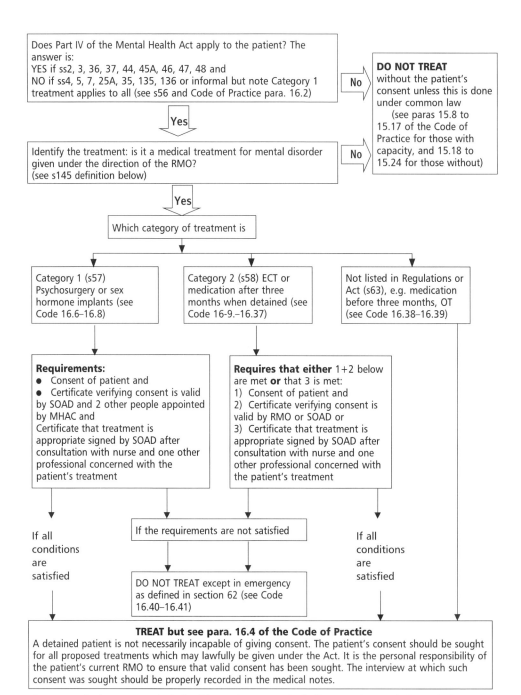

Figure 6.1. Decisions involving consent to treatment – flowchart

From: Basant K Puri, Robert A Brown, Heather J Mckee and Ian H Treasaden, *Mental Health Law: A Practical Guide* (2005). London: Hodder & Stoughton. © Basant K Puri, Robert A Brown, Heather J Mckee and Ian H Treasaden. Reproduced by permission of Hodder & Stoughton.

Mental capacity and the law (including The Mental Capacity Act 2005)

Introduction

There has been considerable attention paid to this subject for over ten years and an Act was finally passed in 2005 with an expected implementation date of 2007. In 1991, the Law Commission published Consultation Paper No. 119 relating to *Mentally Incapacitated Adults and Decision-Making: An Overview.* Paragraph 1.9 of that paper stated that:

> the existing law relating to decision-making on behalf of mentally incapacitated adults is fragmented, complex and in many respects out of date. There is no coherent concept of their status, and there are many gaps where the law provides no effective mechanism for resolving problems. Debate, stimulated by a series of High Court decisions on sterilisation and abortion, has recently focused on the obtaining of consent to serious medical procedures, but the problems extend far beyond this issue.

Some examples of problem areas identified in the Consultation Paper were:

- Consent to medical treatment.

- Disputes between relatives.

- Significant life decisions. Where an adult is not capable of making decisions such as whether to continue living at home, it is not clear who has ultimate responsibility for making such a decision.

- Suspicious of abuse or neglect. It is generally not clear at what stage intervention is justified and who should be responsible for taking any action.

- Young adults leaving care. Despite any mental incapacity they may not be eligible for guardianship under the Mental Health Act 1983 and yet neither foster parents nor local authority will have any continuing legal responsibility under Child Care law.

This section examines some life areas where decisions may need to be taken. It looks at the current state of law. Approaches considered by the Law Commission are outlined and there is a look at the Mental Capacity Act. See Chapter 11 for references to mental incapacity in current mental health law reform proposals.

The 1991 report: decision-making

The Law Commission listed questions that might arise regarding a person's mental capacity to make decisions concerning:

(i)   day-to-day living, such as deciding what to eat, what to wear, when to go to bed or get up, whether to have a bath or a haircut

(ii)   activities involving more risk, for example, going out alone, crossing roads, participating in sports, going on holiday, making new friends

(iii)   major life decisions, such as where to live, whether to enter residential care, whether to get married or have children

(iv)   minor routine medical treatment and prophylaxis, e.g. dentistry, cervical smears, vaccinations

(v) major medical treatment which may have advantages and disadvantages, such as the removal of all of someone's teeth and the provision of dentures, or any treatment where the benefits are evenly balanced and a significant degree of choice is involved

(vi) medical treatment necessitating controversial ethical decisions, such as non-therapeutic sterilisation, abortion, tissue donation, cosmetic surgery, participation in medical research or HIV testing

(vii) legal or financial matters, e.g. claiming benefits, buying and selling property, making a will.

It is not always clear in law when decisions may be taken on behalf of a person who is mentally incapacitated.

Background to current legislation

There is a variety of current legislation which is relevant to these issues but, as noted above, it is fragmented, complex and in many respects out of date. There are some tensions within the law. Maximising freedom and autonomy may conflict with a need for care or control. Again, protection from abuse or exploitation may involve some invasion of a person's autonomy. Another issue is how to identify an acceptable level of risk for an individual. If a professional intervenes without a clear legal base and guidance, they lay themselves open to allegations of undue influence or misconduct. If they do not intervene, they may be accused of neglecting their duty of care. Finally, not intervening may result in other people being harmed or in suffering in some way. If the person causing the harm is seen as 'mentally incapacitated', this raises the question of whether they should face the full penalty of law (e.g. through a criminal or civil action) or whether they should be dealt with differently.

The concept of mental capacity

There is a distinction to be drawn between a legal definition of capacity and incapacity and medical or psychological definitions, though on occasions they will be the same. Paragraph 2.10 of the 1991 paper states:

> *A legal incapacity arises whenever the law provides that a particular person is incapable of taking a particular decision, undertaking a particular juristic act, or engaging in a particular activity. Incapacity can arise from a variety of conditions; historically, these included being under the age of majority, or a married woman, or of unsound mind. Under the modern law, a great many different approaches have developed to the question of capacity based on mental state. Generally there is a presumption that the person is capable until proved otherwise, and capacity is judged in relation to the particular decision, transaction or activity involved. There is also a basic common law test of capacity, to the effect that the person concerned must at the relevant time understand in broad terms what he is doing and the likely effects of his action. Thus, in principle, legal capacity depends upon understanding rather than wisdom: the quality of the decision is irrelevant as long as the person understands what he is deciding.*

This test, however, varies according to specific circumstances.

The current legal position

There are differences in law according to the area in question.

Compulsory admission to hospital and guardianship

The tests here are not of mental capacity but of the person's mental state and the need for assessment or treatment.

Decisions regarding property and affairs

Under section 94(2) of the Mental Health Act 1983, powers of the Court of Protection are exercisable if the court is satisfied, after considering medical evidence that, 'a person is incapable, by reason of mental disorder, of managing and administering his property and affairs'.

Contracts

The relevant test is whether a person is capable of understanding the general nature of what they are doing. The degree of understanding required depends on the nature of the transaction: the more important the transaction, the higher the level of understanding needed. Unless the person is subject to the Court of Protection's jurisdiction, a contract is binding on them if the other party reasonably believed that the individual was mentally capable at the time of the transaction. This applies even if the person was not so capable.

Wills

To be seen as capable of making a will, a person needs not only to pass the basic test of understanding the nature of the act and its broad effects, but also to be able to recall the extent of their property and have an awareness of the moral obligations owed to relatives and others. A person who is mentally disordered may make a legitimate will (even if subject to jurisdiction of the Court of Protection), if it is made during a lucid interval or where delusions have not influenced the disposal of property.

Medical treatment

The basic common law principle is that everyone's body is inviolate. Any intentional touching may amount to a trespass or battery if it takes place without consent. Thus, any medical procedure involving touch, and performed without consent, is a tort. There are a number of exceptions, the principal one of which, in relation to medical treatment, is the doctrine of necessity. 'Necessity' provides a justification for medical treatment which would otherwise be a battery. A doctor is entitled to carry out such emergency treatment as is necessary to preserve the life and health of an unconscious patient, notwithstanding that they are unable to give or withhold consent. Indeed, the doctor probably has a duty to do so. Consent to medical treatment, as a defence to an action for battery, can be effective if the patient's consent is 'real', in the sense that they understand in broad terms what is involved. Doctors may be liable in negligence if they do not fulfil the duty of care owed to their patients. This duty would include, in addition to the obligation to exercise professional care and skill in diagnosis and treatment, an obligation to advise patients, inform them about the treatment, and warn them of any significant risks.

Summary of the Mental Capacity Act (2005)

Background to the Act

1991 Law Commission Report
1995 'Mental Incapacity' (included a draft Bill rejected by government)
1997 'Who decides?' Green Paper
1999 'Making decisions' policy statement
2003 Draft Mental Incapacity Bill
2005 Mental Capacity Act received Royal Assent in April just prior to the election.

Mental Capacity Act 2005 – Defining who lacks capacity – Section 2

For the purposes of this Act, a person lacks capacity in relation to a matter if at the material time he is unable to make a decision for himself in relation to the matter because of an impairment of, or a disturbance in the functioning of, the mind or brain. It does not matter whether the impairment or disturbance is permanent or temporary.

A person is unable to make a decision for himself (section 3) if he is unable to:

(i)   understand the information relevant to the decision

(ii)   retain that information

(iii)   use or weigh that information as part of the process of making the decision, or

(iv)   communicate his decision (whether by talking, using sign language or any other means).

Note: this definition takes that used in *Re. C (gangrenous foot case)* but removes the 'believe it' test which has proved problematic in practice and adds a communication test.

A person is not to be regarded as unable to understand the information relevant to a decision if he is able to understand an explanation of it given to him in a way that is appropriate to his circumstances (using simple language, visual aids or any other means).

A lack of capacity cannot be established merely by reference to a person's age or appearance, or a condition of his, or an aspect of his behaviour, which might lead others to make unjustified assumptions about his capacity.

In proceedings under this Act or any other enactment, any question whether a person lacks capacity within the meaning of this Act must be decided on the balance of probabilities.

Memory requirement

The fact that a person is able to retain the information relevant to a decision for a short period only does not prevent him from being regarded as able to make the decision. The information relevant to a decision includes information about reasonably foreseeable consequences of deciding one way or another or failing to make the decision.

The principles

- A person must be assumed to have capacity unless it is established that he lacks capacity.

- A person is not to be treated as unable to make a decision unless all practicable steps to help him to do so have been taken without success.

- A person is not to be treated as unable to make a decision merely because he makes an unwise decision.

- An act done, or decision made, under this Act for or on behalf of a person who lacks capacity must be done, or made, in his best interests.

- Before the act is done, or the decision is made, regard must be had to whether the purpose for which it is needed can be as effectively achieved in a way that is less restrictive of the person's rights and freedom of action.

Best interests

- Acts or decisions for one who lacks capacity must be in their best interests.

- A person acting for someone else must consider all relevant circumstances in deciding what is in the other person's best interests.

- Regard must be had to whether or when the person is likely to regain capacity.

- The person should be encouraged to participate in the decision as fully as possible.

- Past and present wishes and feelings are to be considered (and, in particular, any relevant written statement made by him when he had capacity).

- The person must consider beliefs and values that would be likely to influence his decision if he had capacity and the other factors that he would be likely to consider if he were able to do so.

- The acting person must consult if practicable anyone named by the incapacitated person, anyone caring for him or interested in his welfare, any donee or deputy, as to what would be in his best interests.

Acts in connection with care or treatment

- D (person acting) for a person (P) must take reasonable steps to establish whether P lacks capacity in relation to the matter in question and believe that P lacks capacity and that the act is in his best interests.

- Such an act could involve expenditure by P.

- Cannot restrain (i.e. use force, the threat of force or restrict movement) P unless it is necessary to prevent harm to P and it is proportionate to the likelihood and seriousness of the harm.

- Where the determination relates to life-sustaining treatment he must not, in considering whether the treatment is in the best interests of the person concerned, be motivated by a desire to bring about his death.

Lasting powers of attorney

- Donor P can confer authority to take decisions on P's personal welfare or property and affairs (or specified matters within these areas), subject to certain requirements.

- Can be made jointly or severally (if not specified will be assumed to be jointly).

- Cannot restrain P unless P lacks, or donee reasonably believes P lacks, capacity in relation to the matter in question. Donee must reasonably believe that it is necessary to do the act in order to prevent harm to P and that the act is a proportionate response to the likelihood of P's suffering harm, and the seriousness of that harm.

Note (s 6(5)): 'D does more than merely restrain P if he deprives P of his liberty within the meaning of Article 5(1) of the Human Rights Convention (whether or not D is a public authority).'

Court of Protection has powers to decide

- whether a person has or lacks capacity to make a decision specified in the direction

- the lawfulness of acts, omissions or course of conduct relating to P

- to appoint a 'deputy' to make decisions on P's behalf

- or, preferably, the Court may make a single order about a matter.

Appointment of Deputies (by Court of Protection)

- Deputies must be aged 18 or over and have given their consent to the appointment.

- May be a named individual or the holder of a specified office or position.

- Deputies can make decisions in areas as authorised by the court.

- They may be paid expenses out of P's property.

- They may be required to report to the court at specified intervals.

Advance decisions to refuse treatment

Possible for people who are 18 or over with capacity who decide that a specified treatment should not be carried out or continued if:

- at a later time in specified circumstances the treatment is proposed, and

- at that time they lack capacity to consent.

Advance decisions not valid if P

- withdraws when capable

- has subsequently created lasting power of attorney conferring on the donee power to make decisions on the treatment in question

- has done anything else clearly inconsistent with the advance decision.

Excluded decisions

- Cannot override Part IV of Mental Health Act.
- Cannot cover marriage or civil partnership, sexual relations, divorce on two-year separation, adoption, plus a few other specific exceptions.
- Voting in public office elections or a referendum.

Public Guardian

- Keep register of lasting powers of attorney.
- Keep register of orders appointing deputies.
- Supervise donees of lasting powers of attorney and deputies.
- Direct visits.

Research

- Safeguards introduced where intrusive research involves someone without capacity to agree to take part.
- Carers will need to be consulted.
- Research must stop if there is any objection or resistance by the person except where what is being done is intended to protect him from harm or to reduce or prevent pain or discomfort.
- The interests of the person must be assumed to outweigh those of science and society.

Advocates

These 'independent mental capacity advocates' replace independent consultees, which were themselves introduced after the Draft stage of the Bill. Regulations will provide more detail on how advocates will operate.

Codes of Practice

- These will be issued by the Lord Chancellor and will contain detailed guidance on assessing capacity, acting on people's behalf and on advance directives. A Draft Code is currently available.

The Act is unlikely to come into effect until 2007 but it is broadly in line with recent court decisions and some practitioners are already drawing on its principles to aid their practice.

Court of Protection and Enduring Powers of Attorney Act 1985

Introduction

The Court of Protection deals with the management of the property and affairs of some mentally disordered people. Its current legal basis is in Part VII of the Mental Health Act

1983 and the Court of Protection Rules 2001. There is a long history of state involvement in managing the affairs of mentally incapacitated people. This was first codified in the reign of Edward I (1271–1307) in the 'Statute de Prerogativa Regis'. The present situation dates from the Mental Health Act 1959. The Court of Protection exists to safeguard the interests of anyone who is, on medical evidence, found to be 'incapable, by reason of mental disorder, of managing and administering his property and affairs' (s. 94(2)). Anyone meeting these criteria is referred to as a 'patient'. The court has wide powers over a patient's property and financial affairs but not over issues of personal care, e.g. consent for medical treatment or to decide where a patient should live. This will of course change if the Mental Capacity Bill becomes law.

Administrative structure

The Court is part of the Lord Chancellor's department. It is an office of the Supreme Court and a court of law, with its own judiciary. There is a full-time Master and nominated judges from the Chancery Division of the High Court sit in the Court of Protection from time to time. The Court's duties are often carried out by appointing a receiver for a patient. From 2001 its administrative functions are carried out by the Public Guardianship Office which has a Protection Division overseeing the work of external receivers, and a Receivership Division which acts as receiver of last resort.

Proceedings

These may be initiated by the nearest relative, doctor, social worker, friend or even an officer of the Court if there is no one else to apply. Legal Aid is not available. The grounds for intervention are set out in section 94(2) of the Mental Health Act:

> *The functions of the Judge under this part of this Act shall be exercisable where, after considering medical evidence, he is satisfied that a person is incapable, by reason of mental disorder, of managing and administering his property and affairs …*

Medical evidence from one doctor will suffice. They do not need to have special knowledge of mental disorder. Mental incapacity must result from mental disorder, as defined generally in section 1 (i.e. it does not need to result from one of the four specific classifications of mental disorder). The appointed receiver becomes the patient's statutory agent. A review can be requested by the patient, either through a solicitor or directly. There is no automatic review of the situation. Fees are payable and these are set out in the Court of Protection Rules 1984. Fees are charged for commencement of proceedings, for various transactions, and there is an annual fee.

Powers and duties of the Receiver

A receiver's powers are limited and specified in the appointment order. A further direction of the Court is needed to deal with matters outside the authority of the order. The Mental Health Act gives the Court powers to authorise almost any legal or financial transaction on behalf of a patient. Commonly, this includes investments, making of gifts and settlements, sale and purchase of property and conduct of legal proceedings. If the patient does not have testamentary capacity, the Court may make a will on their behalf. A receiver is expected to visit the patient at least once a year. They are expected to account to the Court for the management of the patient's property, usually on an annual basis. Some social services departments employ an officer to perform the receiver's functions. Their expenses can be paid under section 49 of the

National Assistance Act 1948. Where a formal authority or directions are needed, but it is not necessary to appoint a receiver, a Short Procedure Order allows this comparatively quickly and inexpensively. This requires only the payment of a commencement fee but, in practice, is limited to cases where the patient's property does not exceed £5000 or where the affairs are very simple.

Comment

The Law Commission (1991, p. 64) has commented:

> *The Court of Protection has in the past been criticised for being remote, inaccessible, slow and bureaucratic. It is arguably unduly paternalistic in its procedures, whereby, for example, the Court's jurisdiction can be invoked on a single medical opinion. The criteria used to define 'mental disorder' and 'incapacity' are said to be imprecise, and arrangements for representing the patient's own point of view to be generally inadequate. Much has been done to improve the Court's procedures and accessibility since 1983 and some of these criticisms are less true now than formerly but the reputation exists and, because comparatively few lawyers or other professionals deal with the Court on a regular basis, there is still a good deal of misunderstanding about its operation. It is perhaps inevitable that the management of 22,000 cases spread throughout the country by a staff of about 300 civil servants based in London will have some shortcomings.*

The Law Commission's 1995 report (Law Com. No. 231) proposed radical reforms and included a draft Mental Incapacity Bill. Note that the 2005 Mental Capacity Act involves major reform of the Court of Protection.

Enduring Powers of Attorney Act 1985

The Powers of Attorney Act 1971 allows a person to put their affairs into the hands of another by means of granting powers of attorney. The attorney may make legally-binding decisions on behalf of the donor. This is fine for many people but there is a problem if the donor becomes mentally incapable because this automatically revokes the powers. The 1985 Act overcomes this problem by creating an enduring power of attorney. A donor is seen as capable of creating a valid enduring power of attorney if they understand, in broad terms, the nature and effect of the document. Thus, there is no requirement that, at that time, they should be able to manage their own affairs. The authority granted by the donor may be general or it may be subject to conditions. Whilst the donor is mentally capable, the power may operate as an ordinary power of attorney. Alternatively, it may be worded so the power only comes into effect if the donor becomes mentally incapable. In either case, when the donor becomes mentally incapable, the attorney must register with the Court of Protection (notifying the donor and specified relatives before doing so). If the power of attorney is registered successfully, the attorney has full power to act within the terms of the instrument and the donor may not revoke or amend this without the Court's confirmation.

One problem with this piece of legislation is that the role is essentially a reactive one as there exists no duty on the attorney to take positive action on behalf of the donor. In addition, the powers are limited to property and affairs and do not extend to matters of personal or medical care.

Activity *6.1*

Sample questions on consent to treatment and mental capacity

1a *What is an advance directive and how might this relate to psychiatric medication?*

1b *What issues may arise if someone makes an advance directive in relation to the use of a particular antipsychotic drug and is later admitted to psychiatric hospital under section 2?*

1c *What difficulties might an ASW face in these circumstances (before and after admission)?*

2a *A patient has been detained in hospital on section 3 for ten weeks and has consented to be on psychiatric medication for most of that period. The RMO considers that a change in medication is now needed and is concerned that the patient may not agree. What are the legal options in terms of proceeding with the proposed treatment in this case?*

2b *Why might a social worker who is working with the patient and their family become involved?*

2c *What dilemmas might an ASW face in these circumstances?*

Chapter 7

Mental Health Review Tribunals. Hospital Managers' Reviews

Summary of provisions concerning Mental Health Review Tribunals

See Chapters 2 and 5 for summaries of when patients and nearest relatives can apply to the Mental Health Review Tribunal and when there will be an automatic hearing.

Introduction

MHR Tribunals were established with the radical provisions of the 1959 Mental Health Act. The main function of a tribunal is to review justification for continued detention, supervised after-care or guardianship at the time of a hearing. In an important judgement in 2001 influenced by the Human Rights Act (*R. (on the application of H)* v *M.H.R.T. North & East London Region* (2001)), the Court of Appeal ruled that a tribunal should express its decision in terms of a positive view (e.g. that the grounds for s2 existed at the time of the hearing) rather than the traditional negative view (it could not see that the grounds did not exist). Sections 72 and 73 have now been amended (see Jones' *Manual*, footnote to section 72). At a Tribunal hearing, an ASW and RMO are likely, therefore, to be asked if they would apply for or recommend detention if they were assessing on that day.

If a patient considers the original detention was unlawful, he can consider an application to the High Court for writ of *habeas corpus* or an application for judicial review.

The main references to Tribunals are to be found in Part V of the Mental Health Act 1983, in Schedule 2 to the Act and in the Mental Health Review Tribunal Rules 1983. (S.1. 1983 No. 942. These are all reprinted in Jones' *Manual*.)

Proceedings in Tribunals can be challenged either by application to the High Court for judicial review or by requiring the Tribunal to state a case for determination by the High Court on a point of law under section 78(8). Anyone who is in contempt of the Tribunal may find themselves subject to action by the Divisional Court.

Key provisions

Section 65 provides for the establishment of one Mental Health Review Tribunal for each Regional Health Authority (see Jones' *Manual* for contact details).

Schedule 2 states:

1.   *Each of the Mental Health Review Tribunals shall consist of –*
     (a) *a number of persons (referred to in this Schedule as 'the legal members') appointed by the Lord Chancellor and having such legal experience as the Lord Chancellor considers suitable;*
     (b) *a number of persons (referred to in this Schedule as 'the medical members') being registered medical practitioners appointed by the Lord Chancellor after consultation with the Secretary of State; and*
     (c) *a number of persons appointed by the Lord Chancellor after consultation with the Secretary of State and having such experience in administration, such knowledge of social services or such other qualifications or experience as the Lord Chancellor considers suitable ...*

3   *One of the legal members of each Mental Health Review Tribunal shall be appointed by the Lord Chancellor ... as Chairman of the Tribunals.*

4   *Subject to rules made by the Lord Chancellor the members who are to constitute an MHR Tribunal for the purposes of any proceedings or class or group of proceedings under this Act shall be appointed by the Chairman of the Tribunal ... and of the members so appointed – (a) one or more shall be appointed from the legal members; (b) one or more shall be appointed from the medical members; and (c) one or more shall be appointed from the members who are neither legal nor medical members ...*

A Tribunal is always presided over by a legal member.

s66   sets out when a Part II patient (subject to civil detention, supervised after-care or guardianship) or their nearest relative may apply for a hearing.

s67   allows the Secretary of State to refer any Part II patient to the MHRT, e.g. if the Secretary of State thinks there should be a hearing before a patient would next be eligible to apply.

ss67, 68 and 76 allow access for any doctor who is acting for a patient in connection with the MHRT to 'visit the patient and examine him in private and require the production of and inspect any records relating to the detention or treatment of the patient in any hospital'.

s68   sets out when the hospital managers must refer the patient to the MHRT.

ss69 and 70 state when Part III patients (those involved in court proceedings) and their nearest relatives have access to MHRT hearings (see grid at the start of Chapter 5).

s71   allows, and sometimes requires, the Secretary of State (on this occasion this would be the Home Secretary) to refer restricted patients to the MHRT.

s72 gives details of MHRT powers. In some circumstances, they must direct the patient's discharge, e.g. if they are not satisfied that the grounds for detention exist. For those long-term detentions where the Tribunal does not have to discharge the patient (i.e. where they have some discretion), they must have regard to:

(a) *the likelihood of medical treatment alleviating or preventing a deterioration of the patient's condition; and (b) in the case of a patient suffering from mental illness or severe mental impairment, to the likelihood of the patient, if discharged, being able to care for himself, to obtain the care he needs or to guard himself against serious exploitation.*

The MHRT has the power to:

- decide that a patient should continue to be detained
- direct that a patient should be discharged immediately
- direct that a patient should be discharged on a specified future date
- reclassify a patient's mental disorder (e.g. from mental illness to mental impairment).

Or the MHRT may recommend leave of absence, transfer to another hospital, with a view to future discharge; transfer into guardianship, or it may recommend the RMO to consider supervised after-care.

If such recommendation is not complied with, the MHRT can reconsider that case and make a further decision.

s77 limits applications to one per eligible person per period of detention and states that applications should be submitted in writing.

If the tribunal confers that it needs more information before making a decision it can:

- adjourn (Rule 16)
- call for more information (Rule 15)
- subpoena witnesses (Rule 14).

Applying for the detention of a patient discharged by a Tribunal

This issue was considered in *R (on the application of H) v Ashworth Hospital Authority*. If professionals think the decision is perverse they should seek a stay of the decision whilst applying for judicial review (see page 35 of Jones' *Manual*, 2004).

Effect of a decision

Significance of the von Brandenburg case decided on 13 November 2003 (House of Lords). Appellant challenged a ruling of the Court of Appeal on this issue: 'When a tribunal has ordered the discharge of a patient, is it lawful to readmit him under s2 or 3 of the [MHA 1983] where it cannot be demonstrated there has been a relevant change of circumstances?'

Facts of the case

On 15 March 2000 the appellant was lawfully admitted to St Clement's Hospital for assessment pursuant to an emergency application made under section 4 of the 1983 Act. The first respondent is the manager of that hospital. The application was made by the second respondent, an

ASW, and was supported by the required medical recommendation. A second medical recommendation was obtained, and on the same day the appellant's admission was converted, again lawfully, into an admission for assessment for a period not exceeding 28 days under section 2 of the Act. On 22 March the appellant applied for a tribunal hearing under section 66(1)(a) of the Act. This hearing took place on 31 March. The appellant's application for discharge was resisted by the appellant's RMO, who gave oral evidence to the tribunal, by a staff-grade medical practitioner working with the RMO, and by the second respondent. The tribunal ordered that the appellant should be discharged with effect from 7 April, deferring the discharge for seven days to allow accommodation in the community to be found and a care plan to be made, including possible medication. On 6 April 2000 the appellant, who had not left the hospital, was again detained, this time under section 3 of the Act. The application was again made by the second respondent. The necessary medical recommendations were made by the appellant's RMO already referred to, and also a second doctor who had supported the earlier admission under section 2.

Extracts from Lords' judgment

It is plainly of importance that the ASW is subject to a statutory duty to apply for the admission of a patient where he is satisfied that such an application ought to be made and is of the opinion specified ... The problem at the heart of this case is to accommodate the statutory duty imposed on ASWs (by whom, in practice, most applications for admission are made) within the principles referred to ... above. The correct solution is ... that an ASW may not lawfully apply for the admission of a patient whose discharge has been ordered by the decision of a MHR tribunal of which the ASW is aware unless the ASW has formed the reasonable and bona fide opinion that he has information not known to the tribunal which puts a significantly different complexion on the case as compared with that which was before the tribunal. It is impossible and undesirable to attempt to describe in advance the information which might justify such an opinion.

Lord Bingham gave three hypothetical examples for illustration only. The essential elements were:

(1)   new information on risk of self-harm

(2)   the patient tells the tribunal that he will take medication but then refuses to do so after discharge, or

(3)   after the tribunal hearing the patient's mental condition significantly deteriorates.

Hospital Managers' Reviews

Section 23(2)(a) gives hospital managers the power to discharge patients detained under Part II of the Act. This also applies to unrestricted section 37 patients.

Hospital Managers have been advised to appoint a small committee to carry out reviews. Panels are made up of at least three members (not employees or officers). At least one member of a panel should be a non-executive member of the trust. The Code of Practice states:

23.2   *The legislation does not define either the criteria or the procedure for reviewing a patient's detention. However the exercise of this power is subject to the general law and to public law duties which arise from it. The Hospital Managers' conduct of reviews must satisfy the fundamental legal requirements of fairness, reasonableness and lawfulness:*

a. *they must adopt and apply a procedure which is fair and reasonable;*

b. *they must not make irrational decisions, that is, decisions which no body of Hospital Managers, properly directing themselves as to the law and on the available information, could have made; and*

c. *they must not act unlawfully, that is, contrary to the provisions of the Act, any other legislation and any applicable regulations.*

Hospital managers have discretion to undertake a review at any time but they must review a patient's detention if the RMO submits a report under section 20(3) renewing detention. They must consider holding a review if they receive a request from a patient and also if the RMO makes a report under section 25 opposing a nearest relative's application for a patient's discharge.

The Code of Practice states at 23.9:

The Hospital Managers should consider carefully whether it is appropriate to hold a review in the case of patients detained for treatment, if there has been a review in the last 28 days and there is no evidence that the patient's condition has changed or a Mental Health Review Tribunal hearing is due in the next 28 days.

Social circumstances reports

Introduction

The preparation of social circumstances reports is a familiar task for social workers but the purpose of these, and the required content, varies considerably. Equally, expectations of social reports have changed significantly over the last 30 years. No longer do social workers and probation officers expect to produce reports with a history of an individual's early childhood and a comprehensive list of psychological and social factors which may, or may not, have a crucial bearing on the issues currently under consideration. Instead, they expect reports to have a clear focus. There have been major changes in conventions on what is acceptable and appropriate to include. Increased rights of access to information have probably hastened these changes, as well as reinforcing the need to base conclusions and recommendations on a proper assessment of available facts, observed behaviour and expressed needs.

The question of making recommendations has always been a difficult one; again, practice has varied over time. For example, in the 1960s and 1970s probation officers moved, over a 10-year period, from a position of not making recommendations to one of expecting to have a significant influence on magistrates' decisions. Similarly, many mental health social workers now make recommendations in Tribunal reports where 10 years ago they were often advised not to do this.

Mentally disordered offenders

The recent focus of attention on mentally disordered offenders brings with it a prospect of greater importance being placed on recommendations contained in social inquiry reports. If a mentally disordered person is convicted of an offence, Home Office Circular 66/90 states:

the court may find it useful to involve the Crown Court liaison probation officer in approaching the health authorities or social services departments in making appropriate arrangements for the preparation of a social inquiry report.

The circular continues that for convicted persons:

It is important that the court should have a social inquiry report available to it in addition to medical advice. The SIR should set out the full range of sentencing options which may be suitable, and give details of the type of supervision and accommodation which could and would be provided in the community. There should be liaison between probation officer, author of the medical report and the offender's lawyer about an appropriate recommendation to the court.

There may be a tension in producing such reports between the need to focus on factors that are good predictors of outcome in terms of offending behaviour, and those factors directly connected to the person's mental health.

ASWs and other social workers may find they are increasingly expected to contribute reports to courts, or to pass information to staff responsible for such reports. The other major areas where social workers are expected to produce reports are:

- assessments for possible admission to hospital
- cases where the nearest relative has made the application for detention (s14)
- general review reports on a patient's progress
- assessments for possible admission to guardianship
- assessments for access to resources
- Mental Health Review Tribunals (and Hospital Managers' Reviews)
- assessments for after-care arrangements under section 117.

Each of these is considered, in varying detail, on the following pages.

Assessments for possible admission to hospital

There are various reasons for completing a report at the time of making an assessment for a possible admission to hospital and many local authorities have an in-house form for such occasions. Information in such reports can be useful for a number of purposes, including:

- providing a record of the circumstances leading up to any decision reached, and documenting the assessment of risk factors
- for hospital staff, in the case of an admission occurring (whether formal or informal)
- subsequent review of the person's needs
- a Mental Health Review Tribunal (especially for s2) or Hospital Managers' Review
- in the case of a compulsory admission, a much fuller account for the reasons for admission than would be apparent from the application form and recommendations.

The process of completing the form can have its own value, especially if this is done at the time of assessment. For example, the form might contain reminders of certain key issues: Is an interpreter needed? Has the nearest relative been contacted and informed of their rights under section 23?

A typical form might cover the following:

(a)   Personal information – name, address, date of birth, ethnic origin, relatives, GP

(b)   Origin of referral (particularly note if it came from the nearest relative s13(4))

(c)   Information at referral

(d)   Interview with patient – their wishes and views (note whether interpreter needed)

(e)   Details of relatives and their views – especially nearest relative's attitude

(f)   Details of significant others

(g)   Medical opinions

(h)   Social, family and personal factors (re: visits by children – see below)

(i)   Alternatives to compulsory admission (informal admission, guardianship, day care, GP, CPN, outpatient care, friends, relatives, etc.)

(j)   Outcome of assessment and positive reasons for this

(k)   * Accommodation

(l)   * Employment/occupation/education

(m)   *Financial position

(n)   *Family history and relationships

(o)   *Community support available on discharge – if being admitted to hospital

(p)   Summary and recommendations for future action.

(*Starred items may be more or less relevant at the time of assessment but may be worth noting in case of a subsequent Mental Health Review Tribunal.)

Some local authorities produce such forms on self-duplicating pads to make it easier for ASWs to complete handwritten reports at the time of the assessment and still be able to pass copies to others such as hospital staff and colleagues.

There are similarities between this list and the factors identified in the Code of Practice as key points to be taken into account when making an assessment (para. 2.6).

ASW reports for applications under sections 2, 3 or 4 (including advice on children)

Paragraph 11.13 of the Code states that the ASW should leave an outline report at the hospital when a patient is admitted, giving reasons for the admission and any practical matters about the patient's circumstances which the hospital should know and, where possible, the name and telephone number of an SW who can give further information.

Circular LAC (99) 32 adds the following suggested approach at para. 9.1:

(a)   *In those instances where a compulsory admission is being considered, the needs of and arrangements for children involved with the patient should be considered by the ASW as an integral element within the assessment. This information should be recorded by the ASW and communicated to the hospital in the event of admission. The ASW should alert their colleagues in children's services if they have any concerns about child care arrangements for*

> *dependent children of the patient. It would assist this process if documents*
> *were designed to incorporate information from this element of the assessment.*
>
> (b) *Similarly, the ASW should provide the hospital with information about the*
> *views of other person(s) with parental responsibility for the children of the*
> *patient, where it is appropriate to do so and if these can be ascertained, ASWs*
> *should be sensitive to situations where the relationship between parents had*
> *broken down so that any decision about child visiting is not used*
> *inappropriately in residence or contact disputes …*
>
> (c) *In the vast majority of cases where no concerns are identified, arrangements*
> *should be made to support the patient and child and to facilitate contact.*

Cases where the nearest relative has made the application for detention

Section 14 of the Mental Health Act 1983 requires the hospital managers to notify the local social services authority as soon as a patient is admitted on an application from the nearest relative on either a section 2 or 3. Then, 'that authority shall as soon as practicable arrange for a social worker of their social services department to interview the patient and provide the managers with a report on his social circumstances'.

It would presumably be good practice for such a report to be provided in cases where the application was for a section 4, but this is not formally required.

Richard Jones (2004, p. 101) considers that the social circumstances report:

> *could include an account of the patient's family and social relationships (including the*
> *attitude of carers), history of mental disorder, previous contact with the local*
> *authority, access to community resources, his employment records, financial situation*
> *and his accommodation. The report should also contain an account of the*
> *circumstances of the admission. If the nearest relative's application was made after an*
> *approved social worker had refused to make one, it is suggested that the social*
> *worker should prepare the report which should include an account of the reasons for*
> *his decision.*

(See also the Code of Practice, paras 2.31 to 2.34, on decisions not to apply and on professional disagreements.)

It is suggested that it would be helpful for such a report to follow similar headings to those used in reports on assessments for admission. The reasons for the nearest relative being the applicant should be clearly stated. If the social worker has doubts about the appropriateness of detention, these should be clearly stated. The responsible medical officer, hospital managers and nearest relative all have powers of discharge under section 23 and the patient may also appeal to the Mental Health Review Tribunal.

General review reports on a patient's progress

These may be designed to be shared with members of a multidisciplinary team and sometimes with the patient and their family. They may contain a summary of aims, facilities and services needed and a review of progress so far. See under 'After-care arrangements' below for typical headings when used with patients who are covered by section 117, and the section on access to resources for some current views on reports.

Assessments for possible admission into guardianship

Sometimes, the same format might be used as for assessments for possible admission to hospital, and, indeed, one could argue that every such assessment for hospital should include a view on the possibility of using guardianship. In many cases, however, where guardianship is being actively considered, there is time to produce a more comprehensive care plan as recommended by the Code of Practice (para. 13.4).

This suggests the identification of services needed by the patient including:

- care arrangements
- treatment and personal support requirements
- appropriate accommodation
- who carries specific responsibilities.

Assessments for access to resources

There is often a specific in-house format for requests for resources administered by the local authority. These have frequently been revised over the last few years as assessment procedures have changed. The DoH/Scottish Office (1991, p. 56) stated that any pro-forma should be used with discretion: 'The collection of unnecessary data can only serve to alienate ... Existing proformas should be reviewed in order to confirm that they focus the assessment on needs.' They can provide a useful checklist to ensure that key assessment need issues have been considered:

1 Has the scope of the assessment been negotiated with the potential user?

2 Has the appropriate setting been chosen?

3 Have expectations been clarified about resources both practitioner and user bring to the assessment?

4 Have the potential users and carers been enabled to participate, with due sensitivity to their ethnic, cultural or communication needs?

5 Have users and carers had appropriate access to advocacy support?

6 Have ... different perceptions of need been reconciled or, if not, any differences recorded?

7 Have decisions on eligibility for assistance been explained to the user?

8 Have the eligible needs been prioritised?

9 Have objectives and criteria for measuring them been set for each of the prioritised needs?

10 Has a record of the assessment been shared with the user? (DoH, 1991, p57).

Mental Health Review Tribunals (and Hospital Managers' Reviews)

Gostin and Fennell (1992, p. 196) noted the crucial role of the social circumstances report for tribunals. 'A patient's social circumstances following his discharge from hospital are at the core of the tribunal's concerns.' They also commented, 'the tribunal cannot reach an informed decision ... unless it has a clear picture of where and how a patient would live if he were to be discharged' (p. 200).

If this information is not seen as sufficient when provided by the local authority, the authors recommend seeking an independent social report.

Part B of Schedule 1 to the Mental Health Review Tribunal Rules 1983 sets out what is expected in reports (other than for conditionally discharged patients):

1.   An up-to-date medical report, prepared for the Tribunal, including the relevant medical history and a full report on the patient's mental condition.

2.   An up-to-date social circumstances report, prepared for the Tribunal including reports on the following:

     (a)   the patient's home and family circumstances, including the attitude of the patient's nearest relative or the person so acting;

     (b)   the opportunities for employment or occupation and the housing facilities which would be available to the patient if discharged;

     (c)   the availability of community support and the relevant medical facilities;

     (d)   the financial circumstances of the patient.

3.   The views of the authority on the suitability of the patient for discharge.

4.   Any other information or observations on the application which the authority wishes to make.

Although it is the health authority who should ensure the provision of reports, it often falls to local authority mental health social workers (including ASWs) to write them, although this is changing in some community teams who give the task to the care co-ordinator. The legal basis for the range of facilities which should be considered can be found in Chapter 9. Note that in the judicial review of *R* v *MHRT for West Midlands and North West ex parte H* (2000), it was held that restricted patients do not have a nearest relative and therefore one should not be named in any reports.

The Code of Practice (para. 23.24) asks hospital managers to ensure that they have relevant reports before they undertake a review. Social reports for reviews should probably be similar to those for Tribunals.

The Department of Health has produced notes of guidance for social workers preparing MHRT reports (sadly with no acknowledgement of the practice of CPNs producing these reports in many areas). These can be found on their website (*www.doh.gov.uk*).

The guidelines are detailed (in the author's view, too detailed) and may be of limited value to experienced report writers. They do give, however, prompts for questions to consider and they helpfully restate the grounds for asking the Tribunal to withhold information, i.e. the information 'would adversely affect the health or welfare of the patients or others'. This is a key area now that the Human Rights Act is in force.

After-care arrangements under section 117

The Code of Practice to the Mental Health Act 1983 (para. 27.19) identifies some key issues when considering after-care and they can be adapted into a sensible list of headings for anyone compiling a report (e.g. the care co-ordinator):

   a)   the patient's own wishes and needs, and those of any dependants;

b)   *the views of any relevant relative, friend or supporter of the patient;*
c)   *the need for agreement with authorities and agencies in the area where the patient is to live;*
d)   *in the case of offender patients, the circumstances of any victim and their families should be taken into account when deciding where the patient should live;*
e)   *the possible involvement of other agencies, e.g. probation, voluntary organisations;*
f)   *the establishment of a care plan based on proper assessment and clearly identified needs, including: day time activities and employment, appropriate accommodation, out-patient treatment, counselling and personal support, assistance in welfare rights and managing finances, a contingency plan should the patient relapse;*
g)   *appointment of a key worker from either of the statutory agencies to monitor the care plan's implementation, liaise and co-ordinate where necessary and report to the senior officer in their agency any problems that arise which cannot be resolved through discussion;*
h)   *the identification of any unmet need.*

Activity 7.1

Sample questions on Mental Health Review Tribunals

*1a When a patient is appealing against a section 3 detention, the Mental Health Review Tribunal has a number of powers at their disposal, as well as recommendations which they can make. These are conferred by section 72. What are the **powers**?*

*1b Identify any **one** of the **recommendations** which the MHRT could make under section 72. In what circumstances might it be wise for the members of the tribunal to make this **recommendation** rather than use one of the **powers** at their disposal?*
(i) recommendation
(ii) reason for use.

2a What powers does a Mental Health Review Tribunal have in terms of making decisions about a patient who is detained on section 2?

2b Why might a tribunal ask an ASW attending a tribunal hearing whether they would be likely to apply for the patient's detention had that person been an informal patient and the ASW were assessing them on the day of the tribunal?

2c   Identify one dilemma an ASW might face in these circumstances and how they might deal with this.

Chapter 8
The Mental Health Act Commission

Overview of the Commission

Mental Health Act Commission	**Chairman:** Kamlesh Patel
Maid Marian House	**Vice Chairman:** Deborah Jenkins
56 Hounds Gate	**Chief Executive:** Chris Heginbotham
Nottingham, NG1 6BG	
Tel: 0115 943 7100 Fax: 0115 943 7101	

The Mental Health Act Commission was established in 1983 and has just over 100 members including laypersons, lawyers, doctors, nurses, social workers, psychologists and other specialists. There is roughly an equal number of men and women. The percentage of current Commission members from black and minority ethnic groups is about 16 per cent. Commission members fall into three categories: there are four full-time Regional Commissioners; an Area Commissioner for each Welsh Region or English Strategic Health Authority (e.g. Dorset and Somerset; or Devon and Cornwall); supported by one or more Local Commissioners. Local Commission members' primary duties include examining statutory documentation, meeting with detained patients and taking up immediate issues on their behalf. Area Commission members undertake some visiting and, in addition, write reports to Trusts and co-ordinate Commission activities across a Strategic Health Authority area.

The Commission's functions are to:

1   keep under review the operation of the Mental Health Act 1983 in respect of patients liable to be detained under the Act

2   visit and interview, in private, patients detained under the Act in hospitals and mental nursing homes

3   investigate complaints which fall within the Commission's remit

4   appoint medical practitioners and others to give second opinions in cases where this is required by the Act

5   review decisions to withhold mail of patients detained in high-security hospitals

6   publish and lay before Parliament a report every two years

7   monitor the implementation of the Code of Practice and propose amendments to Ministers

8   offer advice to ministers on matters falling within the Commission's remit.

The Commission's Biennial Reports (the most recent covers the period from 2003–2005) are available from the Stationery Office and they are a useful source of material about the operation of the Mental Health Act in England and Wales.

Activity *8.1*

Sample questions on the Mental Health Commission

*1a Identify **three** of the main functions of the Mental Health Act Commission which might relate to consent to treatment issues.*

*1b In relation to any **one** of these, what would you see as the likely main strengths and weaknesses of the Commission from a detained patient's point of view?*

*2a Identify **three** of the main functions of the Mental Health Act Commission (**other** than those which relate to consent to treatment).*

*2b In relation to any **one** of these, what would you see as the likely main strengths and weaknesses of the Commission from a detained patient's point of view?*

Chapter 9
Other relevant legislation

Summary of other legislation

The following list is a summary of law which may be relevant to mentally disordered people living in England and Wales. Welfare benefits law is not covered here: information about this should be sought from publications such as the *Disability Alliance Guide*. Acts covering 'community care services' as defined by section 46 of the NHS and Community Care Act 1990 are asterisked * below.

Disabled Persons (Employment) Acts of 1944 and 1958

These Acts established registers, DROs, quotas, sheltered workshops, Remploy etc. The definition of disability was updated by the Disability Discrimination Act 1995 (see below). Section 3 of the 1958 Act enables local authorities to provide facilities for disabled persons to be employed.

National Assistance Act 1948 (and National Assistance (Amendment) Act 1951)
Replaced existing Poor Law. *Part III includes ss21, 29. Part IV includes ss47, 48.

*s21 Provision of residential accommodation for persons 18 or over who by reason of age, illness or disability or other circumstances (including nursing or expectant mothers) are in need of care or attention which is not otherwise available to them. Need to have regard to welfare of all persons for whom accommodation is provided. Section 22 requires people to pay for the accommodation.

*s29 Promotes the provision of a variety of services to disabled people who are aged 18 or over. 'Disabled' here is defined as including people who are blind, deaf or dumb, those substantially or permanently handicapped by illness, injury or congenital deformity, and people suffering from any kind of mental disorder. These services may be charged for.

s47 Removal to hospital or other accommodation of persons who '(a) are suffering from grave chronic disease, or, being aged, infirm or physically incapacitated, are living in insanitary conditions, and (b) are unable to devote to themselves, and are not receiving from other persons, proper care and attention'. Removal must be necessary either in the person's own interests or for preventing injury to the health of, or serious nuisance to, other persons. It is used rarely; if at all, the quick procedure under the National Assistance (Amendment) Act 1951 is usually preferred.

s48 Protection of moveable property: a local authority responsibility when section 47 is used, when someone is admitted to hospital or to Part III accommodation and where there appears to be a danger of loss of or damage to any moveable property and where no other suitable arrangements have been made. Allows right of access to do this and allows for recovery of expenses from the person concerned.

See LAC (93)10 and the accompanying directions about delivery of services.

Health Services and Public Health Act 1968

*s45 Promotion by local authorities of the welfare of old people.

s64 Allows financial grants or loans from health authorities to voluntary organisations.

s65 Allows financial grants or loans from local authorities to voluntary organisations.

Chronically Sick and Disabled Persons Act 1970

s1 Local authorities must gather information on the number of people in their area covered by section 29 of the National Assistance Act 1948 and should inform themselves as to how they should meet these people's needs. Local authorities must also publish information about relevant services. (This provision was extended by the 1986 Act.)

s2 Provision of adaptations to the home and other services. See overlap with section 4 of 1986 Act.

Local Authority Social Services Act 1970

Resulted from Seebohm Report; brought together separate departments and identified legislation which would be the responsibility of the new social services departments.

The Health and Safety at Work Act 1974

This Act stresses shared responsibility for safety. Everyone to accept responsibility for the results of their actions and omissions. The Act sets out the following duties:

The employer:

'It shall be the duty of every employer, so far as it is reasonably practicable, to take care of the health, safety and welfare at work of all [their] employees.' They must provide, 'such information, instruction, training and supervision as it necessary to ensure, so far as it reasonably practicable, the safety at work of ... employees'.

The employee:

'It shall be the duty of every employee while at work (a) to take reasonable care for the health and safety of ... self and of other persons who may be affected by ... acts or omissions at work, and (b) to co-operate with the employer so far as is necessary to enable the employer to perform or comply with any statutory duty.' ASWs are advised to seek out local policies on prevention and management of violence.

Sex Discrimination Act 1975

It is unlawful to discriminate on the grounds of sex (NB sexuality is not covered by this Act).

Race Relations Act 1976 and Race Relations Act 2000

Since April 2001, all public bodies have had a general duty to work towards the elimination of unlawful racial discrimination and to promote equality of opportunity and good relations between different racial groups (s1 of 2000 Act).

Social services departments can lawfully discriminate on racial grounds if the need indicates, e.g. Vietnamese worker with disabled Vietnamese person. Similarly, discrimination is allowed by employers in training (s11 of Local Government Act 1966 provides funding for special provisions).

See LAC 11/77 plus related discussion.

National Health Service Act 1977

*s21 and   Services for the prevention of illness, the care of people suffering from illness
sched 8
(including any form of mental disorder), and the after-care of people who have been suffering from illness.

s22   Duty for SSDs to co-operate with health authorities.

See LAC (93)10 about delivery of services.

Mental Health Act 1983

See separate chapters covering most provisions of this Act.

*s117 After-care services for those detained on long term sections.

Public Health (Control of Disease) Act 1984

s46   Places a duty on local authorities to bury or cremate the body of a person if no other arrangements are being made and gives power to SSD to bury or cremate the body of a person who was accommodated in Part III of National Assistance Act home. A charge may be made for this.

Police and Criminal Evidence Act 1984

This sets out the rights of mentally disordered persons who are arrested and/or charged by the police. The most recent edition of the Codes of Practice, which governs procedures under this Act was published in 2004. It includes details of the appropriate adult role.

Disabled Persons (Services, Consultation and Representation) Act 1986

s1   and other sections concerning authorised representatives are still not in force. Representatives embodied the notion of advocacy and would have negotiated for services and participated in assessments.

s4   Duty to consider disabled person's need for services when requested to do so by the person themselves or by their carer.

s5   Duty to consider disabled person's need for services when leaving special education.

s8   Carer's ability to continue providing care must be taken into account. 'Carer' is defined as someone providing substantial amount of care on a regular basis but who is not employed to do so by a statutory agency.

Children Act 1989 (See also chapter 31 in the Code of Practice re: which legislation to use)

s25   Secure accommodation order applies to children not detained under Mental Health Act where risk exists of self-harm or of absconding followed by harm. No more than 72 hours detained per 28 days period without the authority of the court.

s31   Supervision Order: local authority may specify where child lives, have psychiatric examination, etc.

s31   Care Order: local authority then becomes 'nearest relative'.

s38   Interim care order or supervision order: maximum initial eight weeks with renewals of four weeks.

s43   Child assessment order: maximum seven days. May include psychiatric examination.

s44   Emergency protection order: maximum initial eight days with extension of seven days. May be removed to accommodation or kept in hospital.

s46   Police protection: maximum 72 hours where police believe risk of significant harm; may be removed to accommodation or kept in hospital.

s47   Local authority enquiries – to safeguard or promote child's welfare.

(See *Mental Health Review Tribunals* by Anselm Eldergill (1998) for an excellent summary.)

National Health Service and Community Care Act 1990

Part III of the Act is relevant to social services departments.

s42   Amongst other matters, this section allows SSDs to fulfil responsibilities in the provision of welfare services (e.g. under s21 of the National Assistance Act 1948) by making arrangements with private concerns or voluntary organisations as their agents.

s46   Each social services authority must publish a strategic plan for the provision of community care services in their area.

s47   Requires local authorities to assess individuals' needs if they appear to need community care

s48   Inspection of premises used for provision of community care services.

s49   Makes arrangements for transfer of staff between health authorities and local authorities.

s50   Makes amendments to the Local Authority Social Services Act 1970, e.g. need to establish a complaints procedure.

General power to declare local authorities to be in default if they fail to carry out their functions under the above Acts of 1948, 1977 and 1983. Secretary of State can then direct local authorities to comply, and can enforce this by an order of mandamus from the High Court.

Carers (Recognition and Services) Act 1995

Requires local authorities to take proper account of carers' circumstances when carrying out an assessment of the need for community care services of the person being cared for.

Disability Discrimination Act 1995

This Act requires service providers to take reasonable steps to change practice, policies or procedures which make it impossible or unreasonably difficult for disabled people to use a service. 'Disability' is defined as 'a physical or mental impairment which has a substantial and long-term adverse effect on ability to carry out normal day-to-day activities'. 'Long-term' is a year (or less if an illness is terminal). ' Mental impairment' here includes mental illness.

Housing Act 1996

s182 Requires housing authorities and social services authorities to have regard to guidance issued by the Secretary of State when dealing with homeless people.

s213 Requires housing authorities and social services authorities to co-operate with each other when dealing with homeless people.

Community Care (Direct Payments) Act 1996

Allows local authorities to deliver community care services via direct payments. It aims to give more control and choice to service users.

Human Rights Act 1998 (see the following section for further information)

Commencement date 2 October 2000.

Embodies European Convention on Human Rights within the British legal system. Individuals are able to pursue rights through British courts.

Health Act 1999

Part III of the Act is relevant to social services departments.

s28 Requires Primary Care Trusts, NHS Trusts and local authorities to participate in the preparation and review of health authorities' health care plans.

s31 Provides for the Secretary of Health to issue regulations so that NHS bodies and local authorities can pool resources, delegate functions and transfer resources from one to another if this is likely to lead to improvement in the way functions are exercised. This can link to single provision of services (e.g. see Somerset Partnership). This does not, however, affect legal liability for such services.

These are permissive powers.

- No limit to size of partnerships or number of partners.

- Pooled funds are to achieve flexibility.
- Lead Commissioning (HA, LA, PCT) is where one agency commissions services delegated to it by partner agencies.
- Delegation of functions could lead to secondment or transfer of staff.
- Integrated provision allows better co-ordination of services through one management structure.

Health Act Reg. 6 excludes appointment of ASW from partnerships. In section 145 of the Mental Health Act, an ASW is an officer of a local social services authority appointed to act as an ASW for the purposes of this Act. Jones submits that an 'officer' is 'a person who has a contract of employment with that authority' and notes that DHSS LAC(86)15 refers to 'an employing authority' having the right to withdraw approval from a social worker in certain circumstances.

Local Government Act 2000

Included in this Act are arrangements to create a new framework for local authorities to work with other agencies to plan and commission services for vulnerable people.

Care Standards Act 2000

According to the government, this will help raise the quality of health and social services through new independent inspection arrangements through the Commission for Health Improvement and the National Care Standards Commission. According to the White Paper (2000) on Reforming the Mental Health Act:

> *The establishment of the National Institute for Clinical Excellence and the proposed Social Care Institute for Excellence will ensure the latest advances in clinical and social care practice are spread widely and more quickly. These changes will help to tackle the inconsistencies that have characterised both health and social care services for so long.*

The General Social Care Council replaced CCETSW from October 2001.

Carers and Disabled Children Act 2000

This legislation allows local authorities to provide services and support directly to carers. This can include direct payments. A carer's own needs can now be directly assessed. The Act also introduced a short-term break voucher scheme designed to provide flexibility in the timing of carers' breaks. Any services to carers may be subject to charge.

Two local authority circulars are summarised below: see the 'Race Relations Act 1976' and 'Circular LAC(93)10' below.

See also 'Carers' legislation' in Chapter 3 for further details on carers' legislation.

Human Rights Act 1998

The Act became operational on 2 October 2000. It does not incorporate the whole of the European Convention on Human Rights but it does include the following (*comments in italics refer to some of the possible implications in the mental health field*).

Article 2	**Right to life** Everyone's right to life shall be protected by law. *This might mean entitlement to adequate medical assistance in emergencies.*
Article 3	**Prohibition of torture** No one to be subject to torture or inhuman or degrading treatment or punishment. *Case law suggests this has a fairly high threshold but might be breached by excessive use of control and restraint.*
Article 5	**Right to liberty and security of person** 5.1 No one shall be deprived of their liberty except for specific cases and in accordance with procedure prescribed by law ... e.g. after conviction, lawful arrest on suspicion of having committed an offence, lawful detention of person of unsound mind, to prevent spread of infectious diseases. 5.4 Everyone deprived of liberty by arrest or detention shall be entitled to take proceedings by which the lawfulness of the detention shall be decided speedily by a Court and release ordered if the detention is not lawful.
	*Note that in the Bournewood case (**HL** v **UK**) the European Court ruled that there had been breaches of Articles 5.1 and 5.4.*
Article 6	**Right to a fair trial** Everyone is entitled to a fair and public hearing within a reasonable time by an independent and impartial Tribunal. *The principles of this article are often extended to psychiatric patients covered by Article 5.4. Keeping information from a patient in an MHRT report may be seen to breach the right to a fair trial even if done to respect Article 8. Staff need to be careful about suggesting this and, if doing so, should certainly relate this to the Tribunal rules – see Chapter 7.*
Article 8	**Right to respect for private and family life** Everyone has the right to respect for his private and family life, his home and his correspondence. *There is a dilemma if an ASW is obliged by statute to consult with a nearest relative and this may cause distress to a patient. Consulting when a patient has asked for this not to happen may be seen to breach Article 8. See discussion in Jones' Manual on 'practicability' of contacting nearest relative. He suggests this should be interpreted broadly in the light of the ECHR so that contact could be seen to be 'impracticable'. ASWs may wish to seek legal advice on this. There may be other implications for issues of confidentiality plus the question of children's visits to hospital.*
Article 9	**Freedom of thought, conscience and religion** *An in-patient may have restricted access to be able to 'manifest his religion or belief, in worship, teaching, practice and observance'.*
Article 11	**Freedom of assembly and association**
Article 12	**Right to marry** Men and women of marriageable age have the right to marry and to found a family. *Patient may seek conjugal provisions where detained in a secure ward.*

> **Article 14** **Prohibition of discrimination** Enjoyment of the rights and freedoms set forth in this Convention shall be secured without discrimination on any ground such as sex, race, colour, language, religion, political or other opinion, national or social origin, association with a national minority, property, birth or other status.

Some articles of the Convention's Protocols are also incorporated, e.g. peaceful enjoyment of possessions, right to education, right to free elections.

Advice on implications of the Act

Section 3 of the Act states: 'so far as it is possible to do so, primary legislation and subordinate legislation must be read and given effect in a way which is compatible with the Convention rights'. It does not, however, affect the validity, continuing operation or enforcement of any incompatible primary legislation.

The revised Code of Practice to the Mental Health Act 1983 came into effect on 1 April 1999. Although it was drafted before the passing of the Human Rights Act, the Code does make reference to the European Convention in para. 1.1: 'people to whom the ... Act applies (including those being assessed for possible admission) should receive recognition of their basic human rights under the European Convention on Human Rights'. ASWs may wish to ask for guidance on the implications of this both in specific instances and as a matter of general principle. Managers and legal departments can expect to become increasingly involved in this area.

Public authorities

Public authorities are required to act in a way which is compatible with ECHR rights unless they are prevented from doing so by statute. Advice from the Department of Health would suggest that the following would be defined as public authorities:

- Courts
- Tribunals
- NHS Trusts
- Private/voluntary contractors undertaking public functions under NHS contract
- Local authorities (including social services)
- Primary Care Trusts
- GPs, dentists, opticians and pharmacists when undertaking NHS work
- Bodies with public functions such as the General Medical Council.

The Sainsbury Centre states that the following would probably also be seen to be public authorities:

- Mental Health Act Commission
- Commission for Health Improvement
- National Institute for Clinical Excellence

- Health Service Ombudsman.

Key terms

Absolute rights	cannot be limited or qualified (e.g. Article 3 never allows torture, inhuman or degrading treatment)
Limited rights	specify limitations (e.g. the right to liberty allows for the detention of 'persons of unsound mind')
Qualified rights	sets out when interference with such rights is permissible (where in accordance with the law, necessary in a democratic society, related to the tone of the aims in the relevant article)
Proportionality	interference with rights must be no more than necessary to achieve the intended objective
Living instrument	European Court will interpret ECHR in light of present-day conditions
Margin of appreciation	describes the measure of discretion given to the state in deciding on action under scrutiny (e.g. national security)
Positive obligations	Many articles expect positive action as well as non-interference with rights
Declarations of incompatibility	may be made by higher courts with the expectation that legislation will then be amended to make it compatible with ECHR.

References

Sainsbury Centre (2000) Briefing 12. *An Executive Briefing on the implications of the Human Rights Act 1998 for Mental Health Services,* The Sainsbury Centre for Mental Health.

Wadham, J., **Mountfield, H.** and **Edmundson, A.** (2003) *Human Rights Act 1998* (third edition), Oxford University Press.

Wallington, P. and **Lee, R.** (2005) *Statues on Public Law and Human Rights* (fifteenth edition), Oxford University Press.

The National Assistance Act 1948 (plus 1951 amendments)

Compulsory removal of a person under section 47

Introduction

People may be compulsorily admitted to hospital or to residential accommodation under section 47 of the National Assistance Act 1948 or under the emergency procedures set out in the 1951 Act. These controversial pieces of legislation have been the subject of recent debate. Suggestions have been made for their repeal, amendment or even for their extension to wide use. Age Concern have estimated that about half of the people dealt with in this way are suffering from mental disorder.

The powers may be seen as a way of dealing with long-term neglect or of coping with a crisis. In considering the latter, and referring to section 135 of the Mental Health Act 1983 as well as to the National Assistance Act powers, the Law Commission's Consultation Paper No. 119 on 'Mentally Incapacitated Adults and Decision-Making: An Overview' (1991, p.77) stated:

> These emergency powers are generally regarded as stigmatising and are rarely used. The National Assistance Acts are particularly unpopular and some local authorities have a policy of refusing to use them ... Because applications under section 135 are made by social workers, and those under section 47 by community physicians, responsibility for taking emergency action does not lie clearly in any one place.

Section 47 of the National Assistance Act 1948

This provides for the district local authority to apply to the magistrates' court for a removal order based on the certificate of the community physician.

The subject of the order must fulfil the criteria of subsection (1), i.e. they are:

(a) 'suffering from grave chronic disease or, being aged, infirm or physically incapacitated, are living in insanitary conditions, and

(b) are unable to devote to themselves, and are not receiving from other persons, proper care and attention.

Removal must be necessary either in the person's own interests or for preventing injury to the health of, or serious nuisance to, other persons.

Hoggett (1996, p. 93) states:

> A nuisance in law is something which causes either physical damage to the neighbour's property or a substantial interference with its use and enjoyment. None of this, therefore, suggests that section 47 is simply a way of overcoming the reluctance of an old lady who might be safe or more comfortable in an old people's home.

Seven clear days' notice of the hearing must be given to:

• the person concerned (or to the person in charge of them)

• the person in charge of the place to which it is proposed to remove the person.

• (This would be the District Health Authority for an NHS hospital and the local authority for Part III accommodation under this Act.)

The Court must hear oral evidence of the allegations in the certificate.

If granted, the order allows for the person's removal by a named officer of the applying authority to a suitable hospital or other place so that the person can receive the necessary care and attention through his 'detention and maintenance therein' (s47(3)). The order may last for a maximum of three months in the first instance but may be renewed by the court for further periods of up to three months at a time.

Originally the Medical Officers of Health were responsible for operating this legislation. They, like the relevant social workers, worked for the local Health and Welfare department. Now, as a result of reorganisations in the 1970s, there are at least two and sometimes three agencies involved as well as the courts. The Community Physician works for the health authority. Social workers may work for a county council and the district council has to make the application.

The National Assistance (Amendment) Act 1951

This provided a quicker procedure for use in emergencies and this is probably used more frequently than the full procedure. Under section 1(1) the application must be necessary in the interests of the person and removal of the person must be seen as necessary without delay.

The process is simpler in a number of ways:

- the application may be made directly by the Community Physician supported by a second medical opinion

- the application may be made to a single justice rather than to the full court

- periods of notice required by section 47 may be waived

- an order can be made *ex parte* (i.e. without any notice at all).

An order made under these emergency procedures lasts for up to three weeks. An application to the full court is necessary to extend this but it may well not be made once the initial removal has been made and where the person concerned shows no sign of attempting to return to their own home.

Neither of these powers carries with it the right to treat a person against their will. If psychiatric treatment is necessary, use of the Mental Health Act 1983 is more appropriate to consider. For general physical treatments, the law is unsatisfactory in its present state. The Law Commission has recently reviewed this issue in so far as it involves the question of the mental capacity of the individual.

Comment

There is considerable variation in the use of this legislation between different parts of the country. Overall it is used rarely and, where it is, this probably depends to a great extent on individual professional preference. Age Concern (1986, p. 44) in *The Law and Vulnerable Elderly People* make the point:

> *It could be argued that mentally alert people of whatever age have the right to neglect themselves. If there is evidence of a public health nuisance this can be dealt with under the Public Health Acts. Where elderly people live in unsanitary conditions, action can be taken under the 1936 and 1961 Public Health Acts in England and Wales to clear up the home and, when necessary, a short stay arranged in a residential home for this purpose, if agreed.*

While this piece of law remains, Age Concern recommend using it as a last resort, having explored all possibilities of domiciliary help and having discussed all the alternatives at a case conference. (NB An order does not give authority to give medical treatment to someone without their consent.)

The Race Relations Act 1976 (plus note 2000 additions listed earlier)

Part of) Circular No. LAC 11/77, dated 10 June 1977, issued by the Department of Health and Social Security.

RACE RELATIONS ACT 1976

INTRODUCTION

1.	The purpose of this circular is to draw the attention of local authorities to the Race Relations Act 1976 which comes into operation on 13 June 1977.

2.	The new Act repeals and replaces the Race Relations Acts 1965 and 1968. It gives effect to the proposals set out in the White Paper on Racial Discrimination (Cmnd 6234 published September 1975)

MAIN PROVISIONS

3.	The new Act strengthens the law against racial discrimination and establishes a single new statutory body, the Commission for Racial Equality, combining law enforcement and promotional responsibilities in place of the Race Relations Board and Community Relations Commission. A separate provision of the Act strengthens the criminal law against racial incitement.

4.	The scope of the provisions against racial discrimination is broadly the same as that under the 1968 Act. Discrimination is made unlawful in employment, education, housing and the provision of goods, facilities and services (including clubs). Discriminatory advertising is also unlawful. The provisions are more comprehensive than those of the previous legislation. In particular the definition of racial discrimination is extended to cover nationality, and it includes not only direct discrimination but also the application of unjustifiable requirements and conditions which are technically neutral as between different racial groups but which are, in practice, discriminatory in effect (i.e. 'indirect' discrimination).

5.	Under the new Act, racial discrimination is a civil wrong for which the normal forms of civil redress are available. Aggrieved individuals will be able to seek redress directly in designated county courts, or for employment cases, in industrial tribunals, and will not, as at present, have to place their complaints in the hands of the statutory body.

COMMISSION FOR RACIAL EQUALITY

6.	The Commission for Racial Equality will have general responsibilities for tackling discrimination and promoting equality of opportunity and good race relations ...

THE ROLE OF LOCAL AUTHORITIES

7.	The Government is confident that local authorities will continue to play their part in achieving the objectives of the legislation ...

8.	The particular contribution that local authorities can make has been recognised by Parliament in section 71 of the Act, which imposes a general duty on local authorities to take account of the racial dimension in the exercise of their functions. It requires that local authorities make appropriate arrangements with a view to securing that their various functions are carried out with due regard to the need to eliminate

---

unlawful racial discrimination and to promote equality of opportunity and good relations between persons of different racial groups ...

9. Local authorities have already taken steps to implement the existing race relations legislation as far as employment matters are concerned and have, in general, a good record in this respect. Bare compliance with the provisions of the legislation is, of course, not enough: it is important that employment policies and practices should include effective procedures to ensure equality of opportunity for members of minority groups. Such procedures need to be kept under regular review.

10. The provisions of the Act and ... procedures for enforcement ... are summarised in the attached Annex.

Annex
PROVISIONS OF THE RACE RELATIONS ACT 1976

PROVISIONS AGAINST DISCRIMINATION

1. Part I of the Act sets out the definitions of discrimination. In itself, it does not define what constitutes unlawful discrimination. This is done in Parts II–IV of the Act, which apply the definitions of discrimination to the contexts of employment, education, housing etc. Exceptions to these provisions are contained in these Parts of the Act. There are also general exceptions (in Part VI), covering such matters as provision to meet special needs, and acts done under statutory authority and other approved arrangements, or to safeguard national security ...

2. The exception relating to special needs will be of importance to local authorities in the application of their services to minority communities within their area. This exception provides that Parts II–IV of the Act do not render unlawful 'any act done in affording persons of a particular racial group access to facilities or services to meet the special needs of persons of that group in regard to their education, training or welfare, or any ancillary benefits' (section 35). It is particularly relevant to education, social services and housing. It will, for example, enable consideration to be given to special housing or social service arrangements where for example particular Asian or West Indian groups have special needs. There may include residential home provision for children and the elderly.

3. The Act also permits persons of a particular racial group to be given training for, and to be encouraged to take up, particular work in which no, or relatively few, persons of that racial group have been employed (section 38).

Discussion

The Race Relations Act was extended to cover nationality but does not yet cover religion. The *Guardian* (28 October 1998) noted that the British National Party could attempt to stir up hatred against Muslims without contravening the Public Order Act 1985 on the technicality that Muslims are not a racial group. Sikhs have established themselves in law as a distinct ethnic group, as have Jews, but Rastafarians have not. Gypsies have been given the status of a racial group but travellers have not. Scots are not in law a separate ethnic or national group (*Boyce* v *British Airways* [1997]).There is a useful analysis in Brayne *et al.* (2005) on the practical implications of current legislation for social workers seeking to practise in an anti-oppressive way.

On 18 February 2001 The *Observer* published figures of race-related crimes which highlight a major problem in rural areas with small ethnic minority populations. The table below is based on figures published in the article.

Constabulary	Size of ethnic minority population	% affected by racist incidents
Northumbria	14,700	7.88
Devon & Cornwall	8,900	6.04
Avon & Somerset	25,200	3.52
Dorset	5,800	3.19
Gloucestershire	9,100	2.84
Hampshire	24,500	2.67
Wiltshire	9,200	2.40
London (Met & City)	1,189,300	1.97
West Midlands	287,200	0.54

These figures reflect incidents between April 1999 and April 2000.

Reference

Brayne, H., Martin, G. and Carr, H. (2005) *Law for Social Workers (Ninth Edition)*, Oxford University Press.

Circular No. LAC (93)10 – Services for Mentally Disordered People

Dated March 1993, and issued by the Department of Health.

Approvals and directions for arrangements from 1 April 1993 made under Schedule 8 to the National Health Service Act 1977 and Sections 21 and 29 of the National Assistance Act 1948.

Summary This circular contains guidance on the consolidated approvals and directions made by the Secretary of State for Health on local authorities' continuing responsibilities, from 1 April 1993 to provide residential accommodation and welfare services, insofar as they are provided under sections 21 and 29 of the National Assistance Act 1948 and paragraphs 1 and 2 of Schedule 8 of the NHS Act 1977.

- This circular contains approvals and directions made by the Secretary of State in exercise of the powers conferred by sections 21(1) and 29(1) of the National Assistance Act 1948 and paragraphs 1 and 2 of Schedule 8 to the National Health Service Act 1977.
- It consolidates the existing approvals and directions contained in LAC 13/74, LAC 19/74, LAC (74)28 and Annexes 1 and 2 of LAC (91)12. This circular does not of itself create any additional responsibilities which have not previously been expected of local

▶

social services authorities. This circular also updates existing guidance on registration practice and related statistics.

- Social services authorities' powers to prevent mental disorder or provide care for those who are or have been suffering from mental disorder are embraced in their wider powers under paragraph 2 of Schedule 8 to the 1977 Act to prevent illness and provide care for those who are or have been suffering from it. In addition, if authorities wish to provide services other than accommodation specifically for persons who are alcoholic or drug-dependent, the Secretary of State has approved them so doing. Because authorities' powers to provide accommodation under paragraph 2 of Schedule 8 are being repealed, the approvals and directions in relation to the provision of accommodation for the prevention of mental disorder or for persons who are or who have been suffering from mental disorder, or specifically for persons who are alcoholic or drug dependent, have all been transferred to section 21(1) of the 1948 Act. Further guidance on the provision of alcohol and drug services within community care is contained in LAC (93)2.

Secretary of State's approvals and directions under section 29(1) of the National Assistance Act 1948 *Appendix 2 to Department of Health Circular No. LAC (93)10.*

Powers and duties to make welfare arrangements

2.(1) The Secretary of State hereby approves the making by local authorities of arrange-ments under s29(1) of the Act for all persons to whom that subsection applies and directs local authorities to make arrangements under section 29(1) of the Act in rela-tion to persons who are ordinarily resident in their area for all or any of the following purposes –

(a) to provide a social work service and such advice and support as may be needed for people in their own homes or elsewhere;

(b) to provide, whether at centres or elsewhere, facilities for social rehabilitation and adjustment to disability including assistance in overcoming limitations of mobility or communication;

(c) to provide, whether at centres or elsewhere, facilities for occupational, social, cultural and recreational activities and, where appropriate, the making of payments to persons for work undertaken by them.

Secretary of State's approvals and directions under paras. 1 and 2 of Schedule 8 to the NHS Act 1977 *(Appendix 3 to Department of Health Circular No. LAC (93)10)*

Commencement, Interpretation and Extent

1.(1) These Approvals and Directions shall come into force on 1 April 1993. (2) In these Approvals and Directions, unless the context otherwise requires 'the Act' means the NHS Act 1977. (3) The Interpretation Act 1978 applies to these Approvals and Direc-tions as it applies to an Act of Parliament. (4) For avoidance of doubt, these Approvals and Directions apply only to England and Wales.

Services for expectant and nursing mothers

2. The Secretary of State hereby approves the making of arrangements under paragraph 1(1) of Schedule 8 to the Act for the care of expectant and nursing Mothers (of any age) other than the provision of residential accommodation for them.

Services for the purpose of the prevention of illness etc.

3.(1) The Secretary of State hereby approves the making by local authorities of arrangements under para. 2(1) of Schedule 8 to the Act for the purpose of the prevention of illness, and the care of persons suffering from illness and for the after-care of persons who have been so suffering and in particular for – (a) the provision, for persons whose care is undertaken with a view to preventing them becoming ill, persons suffering from illness and persons who have been so suffering, of centres or other facilities for training them or keeping them suitably occupied and the equipment and maintenance of such centres; (b) the provision, for the benefit of such persons as are mentioned in paragraph (a) on previous page, of ancillary or supplemental services.

(2) The Secretary of State hereby directs local authorities to make arrangements under paragraph 9(1) of Schedule 8 to the Act for the purposes of the prevention of mental disorder, or in relation to persons who are or who have been suffering from mental disorder –

(a) for the provision of centres (including training centres and day centres) or other facilities (including domiciliary facilities), whether in premises managed by the local authority or otherwise, for training or occupation of such persons;

(b) for the appointment of sufficient social workers in their area to act as approved social workers for the purposes of the Mental Health Act 1983;

(c) for the exercise of the functions of the authority in respect of persons suffering from mental disorder who are received into guardianship under Part II or III of the Mental Health Act 1983 (whether the guardianship of the local social services authority or of other persons).

(d) For the provision of social work and related services to help in the identification, diagnosis, assessment and social treatment of mental disorder and to provide social work support and other domiciliary and a care services to people living in their homes and elsewhere.

(3) Without prejudice to the generality of sub-paragraph (1), the Secretary of State hereby approves the making by local authorities of arrangements under paragraph 2(1) of Schedule 8 to the Act for the provision of –

(a) meals to be served at the centres or other facilities referred to in sub-paragraphs (1)(a) and (2)(a) above and meals-on-wheels for house-bound people not provided for (i) under section 45(1) of the Health Services and Public Health Act 19968, or (ii) by a District Council under paragraph 1 of Part II of Schedule 9 to the Health and Social Services and Social Security Adjudications Act 1983.

(b) remuneration for persons engaged in suitable work at the centres or other facilities referred to in subparagraphs (1)(a) and (2)(e) above, subject to paragraph 2(2)(a) of Schedule 8 to the Act;

(c) social services (including advice and support) for the purposes of preventing the impairment of physical or mental health of adults in families where such impairment is likely, and for the purposes of preventing the break-up of such families, or for assisting in their rehabilitation;

(d) night-sitter services;

(e) recuperative holidays;

(f) facilities for social and recreational activities;

(g) services specifically for persons who are alcoholic or drug-dependent.

▶

Services made available by another local authority, etc.

3. For purposes of any arrangements made under these Approvals and Directions, the Secretary of State hereby approves the use by local authorities of services or facilities made available by another authority, voluntary body or persons on such conditions as may be agreed, but in making such arrangements, a local authority shall have regard to the importance of services being provided as near to a person's home as is practicable.

(Appendix 4 on statistics is not reprinted here.)

Activity 9.1

Sample questions on other relevant legislation

1a What is a 'declaration of incompatibility' in relation to the Human Rights Act?

1b Give one example where the government has taken some action as a result.

1c Give an example where the government does not appear to have taken any action as a result of such a declaration.

2a What legal reasons might there be for an ASW seeking an interpreter when conducting an assessment for a possible admission to hospital under the Mental Health Act 1983? Identify more than one relevant statute.

2b What difficulties might seeking and working with an interpreter create in practice for the ASW in seeking to follow statute and guidance?

Chapter 10
Notes of guidance

Risk assessment: Guidance on discharge from hospital

This chapter summarises guidance given by the NHS Executive in HSG(94)27 (this was circulated to Social Services Departments as LASSL(94)4): *Guidance on the discharge of mentally disordered people and their continuing care in the community.* In the following section of this chapter is some material from the revised CPA policy document (October 1999). The guidance is summarised here in so far as it relates to patients who present special risks. Details are followed by a summary of risk criteria contained in key sections of the Mental Health Act 1983.

Introduction

- The guidance is part of the ten-point plan announced by Virginia Bottomley in 1993.
- It links with guidance on CPA and it anticipated the introduction of supervised aftercare.
- It emphasised the importance of co-operation with social services (see *Building Bridges* (DoH, 1995) which provides guidance on inter-agency working).
- The material on risk assessment is part of a broader approach to discharge issues.

Patients who present special risks

The guidance focuses on those 'with longer term, more severe disabilities and particularly those known to have a potential for dangerous or risk-taking behaviour' (para. 23).

23. *No decision to discharge should be agreed unless those taking the clinical decisions are satisfied that the behaviour can be controlled without serious risk to the patient or to other people. In each case, it must be demonstrable that decisions have been taken after full and proper consideration of any evidence about risk the patient presents.*

24. *Before discharge, there must be a careful assessment by both the multi-disciplinary team responsible for a patient in hospital and those who will be taking responsibility for his or her care in the community. Those involved must agree the findings of a risk assessment (see below), the content of a care plan*

and who will deliver it. In accordance with good practice in the delivery of the [CPA] generally, there must be a contemporaneous note of the outcome of any risk assessment and of any management action deemed necessary and taken.

25. *Although the progress of many mentally disordered people after discharge from hospital can be monitored adequately by attendance at an out-patient clinic to see a psychiatrist and/or by visits by a community mental health nurse, this is unlikely to be sufficient for those patients presenting a complex range of needs. They are likely to need regular and, at times, possibly urgent multi-disciplinary re-assessments by the community-based team. Which members of the team need to come together for a particular case will be a matter of judgement, but at least the consultant, the nurse, social worker or care manager and always the keyworker should be involved. The patient's [GP] should be informed in all cases even if it is not practical to involve him or her in the immediate consideration. Where an urgent problem arises, one responsible person (preferably the keyworker or another professional in consultation with the keyworker) should take the necessary immediate action followed by wider consultation as soon as possible.*

The responsibilities of those assessing future risks

26. *There have been a number of cases that demonstrate how difficult it can be in the present state of knowledge to make accurate judgements about future risks. All professional staff involved need to recognise these difficulties and make an honest and thorough assessment based on best current practice and taking account of all the known circumstances of each case.*

Assessing potentially violent patients

27. *Patients who have a history of aggressive and risk-taking behaviour present special problems and require very careful assessment. They pose particular challenges to clinicians who have to try to predict their future behaviour and the risks of further violence.*

28. *It is widely agreed that assessing the risk of a patient acting in an aggressive or violent way at some time in the future is at best an inexact science. But there are some ways in which uncertainty may be reduced.*

Making sure relevant information is available

A proper assessment cannot be made in the absence of information about a patient's background, present mental state and social functioning and also his or her past behaviour. It is essential to take account of all relevant information, whatever its source. As well as the treatment team and the patient, sources may include relatives, carers, friends, the police, probation officers, housing departments, and social workers, and also local press reports and concerns expressed by neighbours. Proper regard must be paid to legal and other obligations relating to confidentiality. However, wherever possible, information that is relevant to forming an overall view of a case should be made available in the interests of the patient. Too often it has proved that information indicating an increased risk existed but had not been communicated and acted upon.

Conducting a full assessment of risk

The Panel of Inquiry into the case of Kim Kirkman (West Midlands RHA, 1991) concluded that the following all played a part in arriving at a decision about risk:

- the past history of the patient
- self-reporting by the patient at interview
- observation of the behaviour and mental state of the patient
- discrepancies between what is reported and what is observed
- psychological* and, if appropriate, physiological tests
- statistics derived from studies of related cases
- prediction indicators derived from research.

* by a chartered psychologist or under the supervision of one

In the words of the panel, 'The decision on risk is made when all these strands come together in what is known as "clinical judgement", and balanced summary of prediction derived from knowledge of the individual, the present circumstances and what is known about the disorder from which he [or she] suffers.'

It is particularly important to know about the past history of risk-taking and dangerous behaviour. As the Kim Kirkman panel again noted: nothing predicts behaviour like behaviour.

Defining situations and circumstances known to present increased risk

While judgements about future overall risk posed by individual patients can be difficult, research has indicated that there are particular situations and circumstances which may indicate an increased level of risk. For instance, one American study of over 10,000 respondents (Swansea *et al.*, 1990) showed that violence was reported more often if drug or alcohol misuse co-exist with a major mental disorder or if a patient has multiple psychiatric diagnoses.

It is often possible to identify circumstances under which, based on past experience, it is likely that an individual will present an increased risk; to indicate what must change to reduce this risk; to propose how these changes might be brought about and to comment on the likelihood of interventions successfully reducing risk. Some examples are:

- when a patient stops medication
- when a person who has previously offended under the influence of alcohol or drugs starts drinking again or enters an environment where drugs are commonly available
- when a person whose aggression has been apparent in one particular situation, e.g. in the context of a close relationship, enters another such relationship.

Seeking expert help

There is a considerable body of expertise on risk assessment within forensic psychiatry. Expert forensic help should always be accessible to local psychiatric teams and should be used in difficult or doubtful cases.

An effective risk assessment will identify relevant factors involved in past violent behaviour, will indicate the circumstances which may influence a patient's tendency to violence in the future and will estimate the likelihood of these recurring. All members of the multidisciplinary team and the patient's formal or informal carers will need to be aware of the results of the assessment. Prompt action must be taken in response to any evidence of increased risk.

Assessing the risk of suicide

29. *Paragraph 2 points out that mentally disordered people are more likely to be a danger to themselves than to other people. Serious mental disorder and alcohol misuse greatly increase lifetime suicide rates. Knowing how to assess the risk of suicide is very important in the successful management of mentally disordered people whether in hospital or in the community.*

30. *All members of the multidisciplinary team should be aware of the underlying risk; factors for suicide and be able to make enquires of patients about possible suicide intent. As one widely used medical textbook (Gelder et al., 1989) put it:*

     The first requirement is a willingness to make tactful but direct enquiries about a patient's intentions. The second is an alertness for the general factors that signify an increased risk. Asking a patient about suicidal inclinations does not make suicidal behaviour more likely. On the contrary, if the patient has already thought of suicide he will feel better understood when the doctor raises the issue, and this may reduce the risk. If a person has not thought of suicide before, tactful questioning will not make him behave suicidally.

     The most obvious warning sign is a direct statement of intent There is no truth in the idea that people who talk about suicide do not enact it.

31. *Two-thirds of suicides have mentioned their suicidal ideas and a third have expressed clear suicidal intent. Most of those who kill themselves have had recent contact with health care professionals. Two-thirds have recently consulted their GP, 40 per cent in the week before their suicide. A quarter are current psychiatric out-patients, of whom half have seen a psychiatrist in the previous week. There are some risk factors associated with particular groups: for example, young Asian women have a suicide level significantly above that of the general population, while among adolescents the most significant predictor in males is attempted suicide (possibly with a mood disorder or substance misuse) and, in females, a mood disorder. The period around discharge from hospital is a time of particularly high risk of suicide, emphasising the need for proper assessment prior to discharge and effective follow-up afterwards.*

32. *The Health Advisory Service is issuing guidance on suicide prevention. This will include more detailed information about risk factors and risk assessment. The Department of Health is publishing the report of a major conference held last year. The Health of the Nation Mental Illness Key Area Handbook suggests a range of ways in which health and social services and other agencies can work together to promote better suicide prevention programmes locally. The first in a series of booklets on mental health for public information and education have been published on mental illness, suicide and mental health in the workplace.*

References

West Midlands RHA (1991) *The Report of the Panel of Inquiry Appointed to Investigate Case of Kim Kirkman*.

Swanson *et al.* (1990) *Hospital and Community Psychiatry*, 41 761–70.

Gelder, Gath and **Mayou** (1989) *Oxford Textbook of Psychiatry* (second edition), Oxford University Press.

Revised Care Programme Approach advice on risk

Extracts from the October 1999 policy document:

Risk Assessment and Risk Management

74.   Risk assessment is an essential and ongoing element of good mental health practice. Risk assessment is not, however, a simple mechanical process of completing a proforma. Risk assessment is an ongoing and essential part of the CPA process. All members of the team, when in contact with service users, have a responsibility to consider risk assessment and risk management as a vital part of their involvement, and to record those considerations.

75.   Risk cannot simply be considered an assessment of the danger an individual service user poses to themselves or others. Consideration also needs to be given to the user's social, family and welfare circumstances as well as the need for positive risk-taking. The outcome of such consideration will be one of the determinants of the level of multi-agency involvement.

76.   Risk assessment and risk management are at the heart of effective mental health practice and needs to be central to any training developed around the CPA. Staff must also consider the extent to which they might need support from colleagues, other services or agencies, especially when someone's circumstances or behaviour change unexpectedly.

Crisis and Contingency Planning

77.   Service users on enhanced CPA will require, as part of their care plans, crisis and contingency plans. These plans form a key element of the care plan and must be based on the individual circumstances of the service user. It is good practice for users on standard CPA to have similar arrangements within their care plans.

78.   Contingency planning prevents crises developing by detailing the arrangements to be used where, at short notice, either the care co-ordinator is not available, or part of the care plan cannot be provided. This could be, for example, the sudden absence of the family member who oversees medication, or the absence of a staff member through sickness. The contingency plan should include the information necessary to continue implementing the care plan in the interim, for example, telephone numbers of service providers and the name and contact details of substitutes who have agreed to provide interim support.

79.   The Mental Health National Service Framework *requires that care plans should specify the action to be taken in a crisis for all people on enhanced CPA. Crisis plans should set out the action to be taken based on previous experience if the user becomes very ill or their mental health is rapidly deteriorating.

80   *To reduce risk, the plan, as a minimum, should include the following information:*

- *who the user is most responsive to*
- *how to contact that person*
- *previous strategies which have been successful in engaging the service user.*

This information must be stated clearly in a separate section of the care plan that should be easily accessible out of normal office hours.

See Chapter 2 for more material on the revised CPA.

Summary of some risk criteria referred to in the Mental Health Act 1983

Section	Nature of mental disorder	Risk criteria to self or others
Guardianship (ss7 or 37)	Mental illness, severe mental impairment, mental impairment or psychopathic disorder. Nature or degree warrants guardianship	Necessary in the interests of the welfare of the patient or the protection of others
Admission for assessment (s2)	Any form of mental disorder (as per section 1) of a nature or degree which warrants s2	Necessary in the interests of the health or safety of the patient, or with a view to the protection of others
Admission for assessment in an emergency (s4)	Any form of mental disorder (as per s1) of a nature or degree which would warrant s2	Necessary in the interests of the health or safety of the patient, or with a view to the protection of others and urgent necessity
Nurse's power to restrain patient from leaving hospital (s5(4))	Any form of mental disorder (as per s1) to such a degree ...	... that is necessary for the health or safety of the patient or for the protection of others
Admission for treatment (s3)	Mental illness, severe mental impairment. mental impairment* or psychopathic disorder*. Nature or degree warrants s3	Necessary for the health or safety of patient, or for the protection of others, that the patient should receive treatment and that it could not be provided unless on s3
Renewal of detention for treatment (s20)	Mental illness**, severe mental impairment**, mental impairment* or psychopathic disorder*, Nature or degree warrants s3	Necessary for the health or safety of the patient or for the protection of others that the patient should receive treatment and that it could not be provided unless detained
Doctor blocks NR discharge (s25)	As per section 2 or 3 – patient is already detained	Patient would be likely to act in a manner dangerous to self or others if discharged
Supervised after-care (s25A)	Mental illness, severe mental impairment, mental impairment or psychopathic disorder	Substantial risk of serious harm to: health or safety of the patient, safety of others, or of serious exploitation of the patient if not to receive s117 after-care services
Hospital order with restrictions (s37/41)	Mental illness, severe mental impairment, mental impairment* or psychopathic disorder*. Nature or degree warrants s37	Restriction order necessary for the protection of the public from serious harm
Police powers to remove someone from a public place to a place of safety (s136)	Appears to be suffering from mental disorder (general definition as per s1)	Person in immediate need of care or control. Necessary in the interests of that person or for the protection of others

* Treatability test applies: treatment likely to alleviate or prevent a deterioration of patient's condition
** Treatability test or, if discharged, patient would be unlikely to be able to care for self, or obtain the care needed, or guard self against serious exploitation

Activity **10.1**

Sample questions on risk

1a *What are the main grounds which need to exist before a person can be detained in hospital under section 4 of the Act? (Do not include any details from section 13.)*

1b *How might the Code of Practice be relevant in the use of section 4?*

1c *How might an ASW be involved if the patient was then immediately made subject to a section 2 and what issues are associated with this?*

2a *What are the main grounds which need to exist before a person can be prevented from leaving hospital by a doctor invoking detention under section 5(2) of the Act?*

2b *Identify one possible misuse of this power and indicate how this might come to light.*

Chapter 11
The Draft Mental Health Bill (2004)

The Draft Bill has been before a scrutiny committee which reported to Parliament in March 2005. An earlier Draft Bill was produced in 2002 and had been expected to be laid before Parliament that autumn. However, it was omitted from the Queen's Speech. It was omitted again in 2003 and was then redrafted in its current form. The Government is still hoping to get the main provisions in place by 2007. The views of the Parliamentary Scrutiny Committee are given in italics at the end of each section.

> *'We have to record that we found the draft Mental Health Bill difficult to read and to follow. We hope that any Bill the Government presents to Parliament will be clearer and easier to read and follow than the current draft Bill.' (Accepted, with reservations)*

The government has responded to the report and its reactions are in brackets. It is now expected that these will form the basis of an Amendment Act in 2006.

Background to review

Report of the Expert Committee chaired by Genevra Richardson and a Green Paper – Reform of the Mental Health Act 1983. Both published in 1999 (Green Paper focused less on mental incapacity).

White Paper published December 2000.

Draft Bill in 2002 drew a largely hostile response from mental health organisations.

> 1. *We consider that the case for reform of the Mental Health Act is cogent but is by no means overwhelming. On balance, we accept that it is desirable for thorough legislative reform to be implemented and we believe it is appropriate that Parliament take the opportunity offered by the draft Bill to set important aspects of mental health policy on a new course for the next 20 years or so.*
>
> 2. *We also accept that the public (including people with mental disorders) needs to be protected from the extremely small minority of mentally disordered people who pose a serious risk of harming others. We fully accept the need to incorporate effective risk management and public protection into mental health policy and a new Mental Health Act. However, this objective must never be allowed to predominate as the primary objective of reform.* (Not fully accepted)

Key elements of the 2004 Draft Bill

- Community Treatment Orders;
- No treatability test
- Broad definition of mental disorder (would include personality disorders and learning disability – no exclusions)
- Mental Health Tribunal and Appeal Tribunal
- Care plans
- Emphasis on compliance with European Convention on Human Rights
- Bournewood and mental incapacity proposals omitted and left to Mental Capacity Bill.

General principles

Code of Practice to set out general principles which must be designed to ensure that:

- patients are involved in the making of decisions
- decisions are made fairly and openly
- interference to patients in providing medical treatment to them and the restrictions imposed in respect of them during that treatment are kept to the minimum necessary to protect their health or safety or other persons.

(But note one or more of these principles may not apply in some circumstances.)

> 9. *We recommend the removal from the Bill of the provision for the possible disapplication of any principles when the Bill proper is brought forward.* (Accepted)

> 4. *We believe that it is essential that fundamental principles be set out on the face of the Bill. It is not appropriate to leave fundamental guiding principles to the codes of practice.* (Accepted)

> 6. *Interference with, and restrictions imposed on, patients must be kept to the minimum necessary to protect their health or safety or the health or safety of other persons.* (Not accepted)

Approved Mental Health Professionals

AMHPs will effectively replace ASWs under the 1983 Act, and the competence required of an AMHP will be broadly similar to that required of an ASW currently. The AMHP role is not, however, restricted in the Bill to social workers, but could extend to other mental health professionals as well, such as mental health nurses and occupational therapists, if they meet the required criteria.
(para. 36 of the Explanatory notes published with the Bill.)

AMHPs will need to be approved by Social Services Departments.

We expect and hope that ASWs will provide continuity in the transition to the new system. And while the AMHP role will be open to other professions, we anticipate that experienced social workers will continue to be the majority of AMHPs when the new legislation is implemented. Other professional practitioners will be eligible to become AMHPs provided they have the relevant professional competencies, experience of working in mental health services and have undertaken relevant training in the responsibilities of the new role. The development and implementation of the AMHP will build on what is best in the existing training and expertise of ASWs so that the independence of the role – which is so important when decisions to use formal powers are made, bringing in as it does the wider social circumstances of the individual – is maintained. We are beginning discussions with providers of ASW training to ensure this happens. It should also be noted that the local authority will be responsible for approving AMHPs – again this will help to ensure that the independence of the role is maintained.

(Department of Health, Mental Health Bill Roadshows, September/October 2004.)

> *102. We conclude that provisions for the move from Approved Social Workers to Approved Mental Health Professionals are satisfactory provided that national training standards are created which ensure that AMHPs:*
>
> *a) bring a separate professional perspective and model of mental disorder;*
> *b) are trained to assess social factors, and have experience in social care and community resources;*
> *c) are equipped to provide comprehensive risk assessments;*
> *d) are trained to explore the least restrictive alternatives to hospital admission; and*
> *e) are trained to manage the practical tasks involved in the assessments and admissions to hospital.* (Accepted)

In the same paragraph the Scrutiny Committee makes a statement which seems at odds with the AMHP role in making a decision concerning compulsion in the first instance (the equivalent of an ASW making the key decision to apply for detention in the first instance i.e. before any appearance before a tribunal):

> *The independent safeguarding function of the current ASW is assumed by the tribunal under the proposals of the Bill, and therefore we do not see the strict preservation of the independence of the ASW as a valid argument for the preservation of the status quo.*

To repeat a passage from Chapter 4, the importance of the ASW role was stated by Lord Bingham in the House of Lords judgement on the Von Brandenburg case when he said: 'I would, secondly, resist the lumping together of the ASW and the recommending doctor or doctors as "the mental health professionals." It is the ASW who makes the application, not the doctors.' The outcome was essentially that an ASW must not fly in the face of a tribunal decision of which they are aware. This, combined with the reversed burden of proof for MHRTs (s72) makes the ASW role similar to that of the Tribunal. Crucially the ASW decision is usually made before a patient goes before a Tribunal and it is hard to see how the Tribunal replaces this in the new arrangements, apart from section 3 applications for patients who are already detained. There will no doubt be further discussion on this point. In the meantime, some may be reassured if the five recommendations about training are followed.

[*R* v *East London and the City Mental Health NHS Trust and another (Respondents) ex parte von Brandenburg* (2003)]

The three stages of examination, assessment and treatment

There will be three main stages which would be the common route for nearly everyone who finds themselves subject to compulsion. This single route approach replaces the various ways people are dealt with currently e.g. section 2, section 3, section 7, section 25A. The three stages would be:

1 Preliminary examination by three professionals (two doctors and an AMHP)

2 Formal assessment and initial treatment

3 Order made by MH Tribunal for medical treatment in hospital or community.

Grounds for assessment – 'The five conditions'

1. The patient must be suffering from a mental disorder

Mental disorder means an impairment of or a disturbance in the functioning of the mind or brain resulting from any disability or disorder of the mind or brain.

(Note the absence of exclusions. The Mental Health Act Commission recommend that the exclusions in the current Act relating to the definition of mental disorder should be retained in an updated form in new legislation, such as, for example: 'no person should be considered to be suffering from mental disorder for the purposes of the Act solely on the grounds of: dependence upon, or recreational use of, alcohol or drugs; sexual behaviour or orientation; or commission, or likely commission, of illegal or disorderly acts, although the presence of one or more above grounds must not be used to exclude the possibility of concurrent or underlying mental disorder.')

11. *Although we conclude that the Government should retain the definition of mental disorder contained in the current draft Bill, we believe the scope should be narrowed by means of specific exemptions and by the conditions for the use of compulsory powers.* (Not accepted)

12. *We conclude that a broad definition of mental disorder in the draft Bill must be accompanied by explicit and specific exclusions which safeguard against the legislation being used inappropriately as a means of social control.* (Not accepted)

13. *We recommend that a specific exclusion on the grounds of substance misuse alone (including dependence on alcohol or drugs) be inserted into the Bill.* (Partially accepted – no compulsion)

14. *We recommend that a specific exclusion on the grounds of sexual orientation be inserted into the Bill. We do not agree that any exclusion should extend to sexual deviance.* (Not accepted)

There are further recommendations concerning learning disability but it should be noted that these were against a background which showed some misunderstanding of the current Act (see page 33 of the report and mistakes concerning grounds for s2).

2. The mental disorder is of such a nature or degree as to warrant the provision of medical treatment

18. We recommend that the second condition for the use of compulsion at clause 9(3) of the draft Bill be amended so as to read the 'mental disorder is of such a nature or degree as to warrant the provision of medical treatment to him under compulsory powers'. (Not accepted)

3. It is necessary (a) for the protection of the patient from

(i) suicide or serious self-harm, or
(ii) serious neglect by him of his health or safety, or
(b) for the protection of others persons

that medical treatment be provided to the patient.

19. We recommend the Government tighten criterion (a) at clause 9(4) in the draft Bill to prevent compulsory powers from being used on a permanent basis in respect of patients who either have a diagnosis associated with a constant risk of suicide or serious self-harm or who engage in chronic risk behaviours. (Not accepted)

20. We recommend that the criterion at clause 9(4)(b) of the draft Bill be changed to read 'for the protection of other persons from significant risk of serious harm'. (Not accepted)

4. Medical treatment cannot lawfully be provided to the patient without him being subject to the provisions of this Part

131. In our view, it is clear that, in accordance with clause 9(5), a patient who voluntarily accepts treatment cannot be brought under compulsory powers. We think this position is ethically correct. However, we agree that issues need to be clarified regarding the position of people without capacity.

Medical treatment is available which is appropriate in the patient's case, taking into account the nature or degree of his mental disorder and all other circumstances of his case.
Note: the fourth condition does not apply to a patient over the age of 16 who is at substantial risk of causing serious harm to other persons.

21 and 22. We note that the definition of medical treatment in the draft Bill is broader than in the current Act, and the Committee therefore believes that clause 9(6) would be inappropriate without the addition of a concept of therapeutic benefit. The purpose of mental health legislation must not be to detain people for whom no beneficial treatment can be found. We recommend that the Government amend the fifth condition at clause 9(6) of the draft Bill so as to include a test of therapeutic benefit as used in the Scottish Mental Health (Care and Treatment) (Scotland) Act 2003. 142. Given the breadth of the proposed definition of treatment, we believe that the number of people with serious mental disorders who satisfy the other conditions but cannot benefit from any kind of treatment will be extremely small. We conclude that people with serious mental disorders who cannot benefit from treatment pose a very challenging problem, but recommend they be dealt with under separate legislation. (Not accepted)

23. We recommend that the codes of practice provide extensive guidance, with examples, assisting practitioners and tribunals in interpreting the notion of appropriate treatment. The codes should also emphasise the need for 'appropriate treatment' to be understood as including culturally appropriate, and that services, as far as possible, should be provided in a culturally sensitive manner. (Accepted)

24 and 25. In the absence of a compelling case to support clause 9(7) the Committee considers it unjustified that patients who accept and voluntarily comply with their treatment should be subjected to compulsory powers. We recommend that clause 9(7) be removed from the Bill. (Limited acceptance)

Initial examination procedure

Each examiner must determine whether all of the conditions are met and if so, if it is appropriate for the patient to be detained in hospital for assessment and, if he could be assessed outside hospital, what requirements should be imposed (e.g. attending or residing in a specified place).

Any person can request an examination.

66. We recommend that the widening of the number of people who can request an examination be tempered by a test or safeguards in the Bill to prevent vexatious, malicious or frivolous requests. (Limited acceptance)

68. The NHS and Community Care Act 1990 already places local authorities under a statutory obligation to assess people who appear to them to be in need of community care services and to decide which of their needs should be met. The evidence presented to us of people seeking help voluntarily, only to be turned away and then committing an offence and ending up detained under the Mental Health Act leads us to recommend that service users have the right to ask for an assessment of their need for mental health care as a resident or non-resident patient, and that the authorities be required to justify in writing any decision to decline such voluntary assessment.

Para. 343. The Committee believes that there is a compelling argument for balancing the draft Bill by including in it a duty to provide appropriate and adequate mental health services which are easy to access and focus on prevention and early intervention.

69. We recommend that the Bill should include a duty on public services to assess and to seek to meet the mental health need of people with mental health problems. (Not accepted within this Bill)

Examiners must consult with any carer if practicable and if patient does not object. For patient under 16, examiners will consult with anyone with parental responsibility.

Duties of AMHP if patient is determined liable for assessment

- Notify patient whether liable for assessment as resident patient or non-resident patient.
- Notify patient of all determinations and reasons for them (e.g. place of residence).
- Notify patient of help from advocates.
- Appoint a nominated person and notify them of the above.

- Register the patient with a hospital within 24 hours of when the patient became liable for assessment. For resident patients the AMHP then has seven days to admit the patient except for emergency admissions when the time period is 24 hours.

Clinical supervisor

The responsible hospital will appoint a clinical supervisor who will be the approved clinician in charge of the patient's assessment and medical treatment. During the 28-day period this person will decide what medical treatment is necessary and whether a further period of treatment is necessary. If so they will produce a care plan to go to the Mental Health Tribunal.

103. *Therefore, in appropriate cases, professionals other than psychiatrists should be able to act as clinical supervisors provided that they meet appropriate standards. We recommend that regulations stipulate the appropriate standards and competencies to be demonstrated following training.* 449. *We acknowledge the inconsistency in the Bill with regard to the prescription of ECT, and we urge the Government to re-consider the issue of whether clinical supervisors with non-medical backgrounds should be able to prescribe ECT, even with the safeguards provided by the tribunal.* (Accepted)

Assessment or treatment orders

Application by clinical supervisor based on the care plan including proposed treatment and description of mental disorder. Clinical supervisor consults nominated person and any carer if practicable. Order made by the Mental Health Tribunal. Could be in hospital or community. Could apply for further period of assessment.

Medical treatment as resident

Tribunal decides if clinical supervisor:

- can discharge
- may transfer from hospital
- can grant leave

or whether these powers are to be reserved to the Tribunal itself. Certain treatments need to be specifically authorised by the Tribunal.

> 75. *We believe that treatments such as psychosurgery should only ever be used as a last resort in exceptional circumstances, and then only under the best possible safeguards. We recommend that Type A treatments at clauses 191 to 195 of the draft Bill be under no circumstances used for patients lacking capacity, not even with the consent of the High Court. Where the patient has capacity we recommend that Type A treatment only be given with the patient's informed consent and furthermore that, given the nature of these procedures, Type A treatments be subject to the ratification of a tribunal, even if the patient is able to give informed consent.* (Limited acceptance)

> 77. *For that reason we believe it is essential that the Bill should set clear limits for ECT administered in emergency situations. Where a course of electroconvulsive therapy is prescribed under the emergency procedure, we recommend that the Bill specify the maximum number of treatments which can be given, to prevent emergency*

treatments becoming a route to a full course of treatment and bypassing the general requirements on ECT. We recommend that the maximum number of treatments under emergency procedures be limited to two. (Limited acceptance)

78. We recommend that the Bill transfer to the new Expert Panel the safeguarding function of the current second-opinion doctor (SOAD) system, which includes the power to veto proposed treatment. (Limited acceptance)

Non-resident patients (community treatment orders)

Order must specify requirements. Tribunal must recommend what clinical supervisor should do if patient fails to comply or there is a change of circumstance. Tribunal decides if clinical supervisor can suspend requirements or if this is left to Tribunal.

30. We recommend that the use of non-residential treatment under compulsion be explicitly limited to a clearly defined and clinically identifiable group of patients. (Not accepted)

33. The following parameters for the use of non-residential compulsory powers should be included on the face of the Bill. a) A non-residential order should not normally be imposed without previous hospitalisation at least for the purposes of assessment. b) There exists evidence of previous responsiveness to, and co-operation with, proposed treatment before a non-residential order is imposed. c) Provisions for non-residential orders should be simple and be used to specify only: requirements or limitations on a person's place of residence; and medical treatment. d) There must be a maximum time limit for treatment under a non-residential order – certainly of not more than three years in any five year period. e) The non-residential order must not authorise the use of force on the patient in the community (i.e. outside hospitals or clinics) beyond the powers currently available in the 1983 Act which provide for a patient to be conveyed to the place he is required to attend for treatment or to be conveyed to hospital. (Limited acceptance)

34. We recommend that the provisions for non-residential orders be accompanied by a requirement on health and local authorities to provide adequate care. Further, adequate care means care other than that provided by families and carers, and any provision for non-residential orders must ensure that burdens are not placed upon families and carers that would fall more properly on clinicians and the health and social services. (Not accepted)

Community requirements may include that patient should:
- attend at specified place and times
- reside at specified place
- make himself available for treatment during specified periods
- not engage in specified conduct.

Treatment for non-residents

Tribunal may authorise medical treatment and clinical supervisor may require patient then to comply, and if patient does not comply, clinical supervisor may require patient to become 'resident' till end of period. Patient may then be conveyed to hospital and detained.

Mental Health Tribunal

Appointment by Lord Chancellor: legal members; clinical members; general members; assisted by expert panel. Occasionally presidents may sit alone. Mental Health Appeal Tribunal to deal with appeals on Tribunal decisions on points of law.

55. *We recommend that the Government expedite the completion of its studies into the expected length of hearings under the Bill, taking into account the concerns we have raised regarding the extended remit of the tribunals and consulting the tribunals and representative user groups. Once these studies are complete, we expect the Government to recalculate and re-publish the workforce and funding implications of the new system in the Regulatory Impact Assessment when it presents the Bill proper to Parliament.* (Accepted)

58. *We recommend that, in the interests of ensuring that hearings are both fair and seen to be fair, there be a clearer distinction between the roles of the tribunals as a detaining body and as a review tribunal. So, for example, a member of a tribunal that has imposed an order for assessment or treatment should never hear the review or appeal of that order.* (Not accepted)

59. *We recommend that the current discretion in section 72 of the 1983 Act, which permits the Mental Health Review Tribunal to discharge patients even where the detention criteria are met, be included in the Bill.* (Not accepted – and point seemingly not understood)

Mental Health Act Commission

The Draft Bill recommends abolishing the Mental Health Act Commission and replacing it with the Commission for Healthcare Audit and Inspection (CHAI). There would not be a focus on the current visiting function.

Para. 330. We consider that the list of tasks suggested by Professor Eldergill has much to commend it, with the exception of the proposal that the codes of conduct should be published by the monitoring body. (We believe that the power to produce the codes should remain with the Secretary of State and the National Assembly for Wales.)

62. *We recommend that the Bill set out powers and duties that will ensure the preservation of a specialised system to monitor patients subject to compulsion.* (Limited acceptance)

In doing so, we suggest that the Government pay particular attention to the duties proposed by Professor Eldergill, save the proposal relating to the codes of practice. This includes duties in relation to all patients subject to the powers in the Bill, including restricted patients.

63. *We recommend, too, that the body charged with monitoring patients subject to compulsion have a duty similar to the visiting duty already imposed on the Mental Health Act Commission. That role includes a duty to visit routinely mental health facilities to interview patients.* (Limited acceptance)

In addition, we see no reason why the responsibilities of the Mental Health Act Commission should not include investigating and reporting on the Secretary of State's management of restricted patients.

64. We recommend that the responsibilities of the reformed Mental Health Act Commission include investigating and reporting on the Secretary of State's management of restricted patients. (Not accepted)

334. We agree that the nature and extent of the functions that need to be carried out make it impractical for CHAI to perform them. It seems to us almost inevitable that, once the duties to monitor mental health legislation are subsumed into a large healthcare organisation, they will be diluted. Experience shows that mental health services rarely do well in competition for resources and attention. It is vital that, if the monitoring of compulsory powers is to be effective, patients know who is doing it and how they are doing it. This is more likely to be the case if there is a focused stand-alone body with a high profile and clear title.

65. We recommend that the powers set out in paragraphs 329 and 330 above be given to a reformed Mental Health Act Commission. In order to take on the new powers, the new Commission will need more resources. (Limited acceptance)

Care plans

These would become a statutory requirement.

73. We recommend that, in the interests of safeguarding patients' rights and involving the patient in his own treatment, the care plan be discussed with him. Except in those cases where the patient does not have capacity, the patient should be asked to sign the plan to prove that he has seen and discussed it, indicating whether he agrees with it. If the patient disagrees with specific aspects of the plan, this should be indicated on the plan either by the patient or the clinical supervisor prior to the patient signing the plan. (Limited acceptance)

74. We recommend that the Bill as introduced place an obligation on health authorities and local authorities to provide the care specified in a patient's care plan, provided that it is in line with normally accepted national standards. (Not accepted)

After-care

The Draft Bill proposes that services should be free while a person is subject to compulsion and then for a limited period of a few weeks.

70. We recommend that there be a duty on health and local authorities in each case to draw up a discharge plan and to provide the care in the plan, and that the provisions of section 117 of the Mental Health Act 1983, relating to free after-care based on need, be included in the Bill proper when introduced. (Limited acceptance)

Removal to place of safety

Provisions of section 135 of Mental Health Act 1983 virtually unchanged.

Section 136 of MH Act the same except that Police may also enter premises in urgent cases on advice from AMHP to prevent serious harm to self or others.

Nominated person

Replaces nearest relative of 1983 Act.

Usually selected by patient.

Where AMHP has to choose, consider from a list and rules which are set out.

Nominated person to express what appear to him to be patient's wishes and feelings about treatment.

91. *We recommend that the nominated person have broadly the same rights and powers currently exercised by the nearest relative under the 1983 Act. In particular, the nominated person should be able to:*

    a) *make an order for the discharge in respect of a patient where the patient is liable to be detained in a hospital in pursuance of an application for admission to hospital, and*

    b) *make an order for the discharge of a patient who is detained in a hospital, subject to 72 hours' notice. The clinical supervisor would then be able to block discharge by certifying that, if discharged, the patient would be likely to act in a manner dangerous to himself or to others. If that happens, the patient, carer or nominated person should have a right to appeal to the Mental Health Tribunal for discharge on the same basis as patients detained for assessment.* (Not accepted)

92. *We recommend that patients be able to appoint an enduring nominated person. This could be done through an advance statement, as explained in Chapter 4, if the Government brings forward proposals for advance statements or, if it does not, through a simple process and free-standing instrument.* (Limited acceptance)

94. *We recommend that, where the patient lacks capacity to appoint a nominated person and has not nominated someone previously, there be a default provision along the lines of the Scottish Act whereby the carer is the default first choice with the nearest relative as the default second choice.*

95. *There was concern among some witnesses about the ability of mental health professionals to judge a person unsuitable to be a nominated person. We recommend that, to safeguard the interests and autonomy of the person under compulsion, the Approved Mental Health Professional be able to disqualify a person's choice of nominated person only if the nominated person is exploitative or lacks capacity.* (Limited acceptance of 94 and 95 – details to be in Code of Practice)

Nominated person's role

To be notified of assessments.

Consulted before care plan prepared.

Consulted before an application is made to the Tribunal for an order.

May apply to Tribunal for discharge.

Consulted on some treatment matters.

Has access to advocate.

Mental health advocates

Available to patients and nominated persons, defined in Regulations.

Help obtain information on medical treatment, why it is being given and under what authority; identify what rights can be exercised.

May meet with patient in private and inspect any records kept by clinical supervisor.

> 83. *We recommend that, before the Government introduces the Bill proper to Parliament, it review the costs of setting up a discrete mental health advocacy service, as distinct from the new advocacy function to be introduced under the Mental Capacity Bill 2004. This review should be undertaken in consultation with those providing advocacy services and the Regulatory Impact Assessment should be expanded to ensure that it reflects detailed and robust costings, and a sensitivity analysis taking account of, for example, possible variations in the number of persons detained and the provision of advocacy services at examination stage, to 'voluntary' patients and to those under compulsion in the community.* (Accepted, with reservations)

> 85. *We recommend that the Bill charge the Mental Health Act Commission with duties to set national standards for mental health advocates, provide accreditation and to investigate complaints.* (Not accepted)

> 90. *We recommend that the independent mental health advocate have no access to patient records without the patient's informed consent and, for people whose decision-making is impaired, the nominated person be asked to make the decision for the patient.* (Accepted)

Definition of carer

A person who provides a substantial amount of care to the patient on a regular basis (or intends to provide such care). This excludes under a paid contract to provide care and volunteers for voluntary organisations.

> 96. *Clause 12(2) provides that carers cannot be consulted without first ascertaining the patient's wishes and feelings, unless it is inappropriate or impractical to do so. We recommend this be strengthened so as to contain a presumption to consult a patient's carer when examinations and assessments are carried out, unless the patient is expressly opposed to it.* (Not accepted)

Children

The Draft Bill contains a number of changes to the position for those under 18.

37. We recommend that the Bill stipulate that under 18 year olds should be accommodated in age-appropriate facilities. This requirement could be modelled on section 23 of the Mental Health (Care and Treatment) (Scotland) Act 2003. If in exceptional circumstances under 18 year olds are treated on adult wards, the Bill should require the clinical supervisor to obtain advice from a Child and Adolescent Mental Health Services specialist during both the assessment and treatment of the patient in question. (Limited acceptance)

Patients concerned in criminal proceedings

This summary will not attempt to address this issue. Essentially the Draft Bill attempts to have a similar approach to civil and criminal patients.

45. We recommend that the Government give serious consideration to ways of improving the drafting so that the provisions of the whole Bill, and particularly Part 3, can be more easily understood, and can be read easily in conjunction with the Criminal Justice Act 2003. (Accepted, with reservations)

48. We recommend that, when courts are considering whether to make a mental health order or hospital direction, there be a requirement that the mental disorder of the offender/patient should be of a nature or degree which makes treatment under compulsory powers appropriate. If the offender/patient is to be resident, then the disorder should be of a nature or degree warranting detention. (Not accepted)

Conclusion

The Parliamentary Scrutiny Committee comments are comprehensive and, if followed, would involve considerable changes to the drafting of the Bill. The government's response suggests they are only willing to consider very limited changes. At the time of this Guide going to print a number of detailed responses from interested parties were available on *www.markwalton.net* and they provide a useful critique of the proposals as well as a commentary on the new Bournewood Gap. This appears to exist in the current drafting of the Mental Health and Mental Capacity Bills as far as mentally incapacitated compliant patients are concerned, and it will need some attention. To refer to the views of the Parliamentary Scrutiny Committee:

182. We welcome assurances from the Government that additional safeguards will be provided for compliant incapacitated patients who are treated informally. Although the safeguards in Part 5 of the 2002 draft Mental Health Bill would, to some extent, assist in closing the Bournewood Gap, we agree with the opinion of the JCHR that they fail to protect all patients in the position of the patient in HL v UK.

29. We urge the Government to bring forward a comprehensive and universal set of proposals to deal with hospitalisation and treatment of patients affected by the Bournewood judgment, either as amendments to a Mental Capacity Bill (as it appears to be intending now), or, failing that, by introducing proposals in the Mental Health Bill, as soon as possible. (Accepted)

169. *Although we recognise that defining the boundaries between the operation of the two regimes will be a complex and challenging task, we consider it imperative that the interface is made clear.*

27. *Accordingly, we recommend that, before Parliament is asked to assent to the Mental Health Bill, a clearer analysis of the interrelation between the two pieces of legislation be presented. The relationship between the Mental Capacity Bill and a future Mental Health Bill should be clarified primarily so that clinicians have a clear understanding of their application in each particular case. This could conveniently be a common part of the respective codes of practice.* (Accepted)

At the end of 2005 a revised Mental Health Bill had still not appeared and there must be a strong possibility that its unpopularity and poor drafting has finally killed it off in its current form. However, the government is still committed to the key elements within the Draft Bill and it may well be that a different approach is adopted. A series of separate amendments to the existing Mental Health Act 1983 could introduce many of the proposed changes. Some, such as the new Mental Health Tribunal system, would take many years to bring into effect but others could be introduced fairly quickly. For Approved Social Workers this could include removing the requirement that they should be officers of the local authority and possibly even that they should be social workers. In the meantime the Scottish Act has been implemented (together with their new mental capacity legislation) and it might be beneficial to look at the effect of these changes. Finally a more radical approach could be taken by going back to basics and asking the Law Commission to review current law and make recommendations for change.

Appendix 1
Checklists

Applications for Compulsory Hospital Admission or Guardianship

YOU SHOULD BE ABLE TO ANSWER 'YES' TO ALL THE NUMBERED QUESTIONS OR BE ABLE TO FOLLOW THE INSTRUCTIONS. YOU MAY ALSO FIND HELPFUL THE GENERAL POINTS WHICH ARE PRINTED AT THE END OF SECTION 4, ADMISSIONS.

Important: Forms 2, 3, 4, 7, 9, 10, 11, 12, 14, 15, 21, 11, 14, 128, 29 and 30 were all amended in 1996. Ensure you use current versions of the forms.

SECTION 2 – Admission for assessment (lasting for up to 28 days)

(1) Are you of the opinion 'having regard to any wishes expressed by relatives of the patient or any other relevant circumstances' that your making an application would be necessary or proper?

(2) Have you interviewed the patient 'in a suitable manner'?

(3) Are you satisfied that 'detention in a hospital is in all the circumstances of the case the most appropriate way of providing the care and medical treatment of which the patient stands in need'? Have you considered and decided against: informal admission, out-patient treatment, community psychiatric nursing support, crisis intervention centres, primary health-care support, local authority social services or private provision, support from friends, relatives or voluntary organisations?

(4) Have you got two medical recommendations, which state that the patient is suffering from mental disorder 'of a nature or degree which warrants detention in hospital for assessment' and that he ought to be detained 'in the interests of his own health or safety or with a view to the protection of other persons'?

(5) Has one of the doctors had previous acquaintance with patient? If not, every effort should be made to find one who has. If unsuccessful, you must give your reasons at the bottom of Form 2.

(6) Has one doctor been approved as having special experience in psychiatry? See your local list of section 12 approved doctors.

(7) Have you seen the patient within the last 14 days?

(8) Have the doctors personally examined the patient together or within five days of each other? (This means five clear days so one on the first and the other on the seventh is acceptable.)

(9) Do neither or only one of the doctors work in the hospital to which the patient will be admitted? If no, see section 12(4), which gives the exception where delay would involve serious risk and where other safeguards exist.

(10) Have you checked the validity of the medical recommendations (e.g. that they have been signed and are from doctors entitled to make recommendations)? If not, and a serious mistake has been made, you could be notified and have to make a new application. Less important mistakes (e.g. spelling of names) can be corrected within 14 days of the admission. (See s15 for more information if needed.)

(11) Have you informed the nearest relative that the application is to be made and of their rights of discharge under section 23(2)(a)? If not, you must do so after the admission if this is practicable. Inform the hospital when you have done this.

(12) Are the dates of the signatures of both medical recommendations on or before the date of your application?

(13) After signing an application you have 14 days to get the patient admitted to hospital beginning with the date when the patient was last examined for the purpose of making one of the medical recommendations. You have the authority to remove compulsorily the patient to hospital and/or to authorise anyone else to do this but should have the recommendations and application to hand to demonstrate this.

Forms required. Application on Form 2 (nearest relative would use Form 1 and a social worker would subsequently prepare a report). Recommendation on Form 3 (joint) or Form 4.

Note: If the request for an application to be considered came from the nearest relative and you have decided against it, you must given them your reasons in writing.

SECTION 3 – Admission for treatment (lasting up to six months and renewable)

(1) Are you of the opinion 'having regard to any wishes expressed by relatives of the patient or any other relevant circumstances' that your making an application would be necessary or proper?

(2) Have you interviewed the patient 'in a suitable manner'?

(3) Are you satisfied that 'detention in a hospital is in all the circumstances of the case the most appropriate way of providing the care and medical treatment of which the patient stands in need'? Have you decided against: informal admission, out-patient treatment, CPN support, crisis intervention centres, LA social services or private provision, support from primary health-care, friends, relatives or voluntary organisations?

(4) Have you got two medical recommendations, on one form or two, which state the patient is suffering from a specified mental disorder 'of a nature or degree which makes it appropriate for him to receive medical treatment in a hospital' and 'it is necessary for the health or safety of the patient or for the protection of other persons that he should receive such treatment and it cannot be provided unless he is detained under this section'?

(5) Does your application specify at least one of the following forms of mental disorder *and* is this common to *both* medical recommendations: mental illness, severe mental impairment, psychopathic disorder or mental impairment? If not, the application will be invalid and a new one will have to be made.

(6) If the disorder specified is psychopathic disorder or mental impairment, have the doctors stated in their recommendations that medical treatment in a hospital 'is likely to alleviate or prevent a deterioration of his condition'?

(7) Has one doctor had previous acquaintance with patient? If not, every effort should be made to find one who has. If unsuccessful you must give reasons on Form 9.

(8) Has one doctor been approved as having special experience in psychiatry? See your local list of section 12 approved doctors.

(9) Have you seen the patient within the last 14 days?

(10) Have the doctors personally examined the patient together or within five days of each other? (This means five clear days so one on the first and the other on the seventh is acceptable.)

(11) Do neither or only one of the doctors work in the hospital to which the patient will be admitted? If no, see section 12(4) which gives the exception where delay would involve serious risk and where other safeguards exist.

(12) Have you checked the validity of the medical recommendations (e.g. they are signed and are from doctors entitled to make them)? If not, and a serious mistake is made, you could be notified and have to make a new application. Less serious errors (e.g. spelling of names) can be corrected within 14 days of admission. (See s15 for more information.)

(13) Have you consulted the nearest relative and checked that they have no objection to an application? If you have not, would you say this was not reasonably practicable or would have involved unreasonable delay? (If unable to consult the nearest relative, you need to see them as soon as possible to let them know their rights of discharge. Inform the hospital when you have done this. See discussion on confidentiality in Chapter 3 if patient objects to contact.)

(14) Are the dates by both doctors' signatures on or before the date of your application?

(15) After signing an application you have 14 days to get the patient admitted to hospital beginning with the date when the patient was last examined for the purpose of making one of the medical recommendations. You have the authority to remove compulsorily the patient to hospital and/or to authorise anyone else to do this but should have the recommendations and application to hand to demonstrate this.

Forms required: Application on Form 9 (nearest relative would use Form 8 and a social worker would subsequently prepare a report). Recommendation on Form 10 (joint) or Form 11.

Note: If the request for an application to be considered came from the nearest relative and you have decided against it you must give them your reasons in writing.

SECTION 4 – Admission for assessment in cases of emergency (lasts up to 72 hours)

(1) Are you of the opinion 'having regard to any wishes expressed by relatives of the patient or another relevant circumstances' that your making an application would be necessary or proper?

(2) Have you interviewed the patient 'in a suitable manner'?

(3) Are you satisfied that 'detention in hospital is in all the circumstances of the case the most appropriate way of providing the care and medical treatment of which the patient stands in need'? Have you considered: informal admission, out-patient treatment, community nursing support, crisis intervention centres, primary health care support, local authority social services or private provision, support from friends, relatives or voluntary organisations?

(4) Is it of urgent necessity the patient be admitted and detained in hospital for assessment?

(5) Would obtaining a second recommendation to meet the needs of section 2 involve undesirable delay?

(6) Have you got a medical recommendation which states 'that this patient is suffering from mental disorder of a nature or degree which warrants the patient's detention in a hospital for assessment' and 'ought to be so detained' in the interests of the patient's own health or safety or with a view to the protection of other persons?

(7) Has the doctor had previous acquaintance with the patient? If not, is it genuinely not practicable to find such a doctor? If unsuccessful you must give your reasons at the bottom of Form 6.

(8) Do the details on the medical recommendation correspond with those on your application?

(9) Have you and the doctor both seen the patient in the last 24 hours? (For s4 you can sign your form before or after the doctor signs a recommendation. Eldergill supports this view, Jones (p. 60) does not.)

(10) After signing an application, you have 24 hours to get the patient admitted to hospital beginning with the time when the patient was examined for the purpose of making the medical recommendation. You have the authority to compulsorily remove the patient to hospital and/or to authorise anyone else to do this but should have the recommendation and application to hand to demonstrate this.

Forms required. Application on Form 6 (nearest relative would use Form 5 and if there were a conversion to section 2, through the provision of an additional medical recommendation, a social worker would probably prepare a report). Recommendation on Form 7.

Note: If the request for an application to be considered came from the nearest relative and you have decided against it, you must given them your reasons in writing.

General points for admissions to hospital from the community

If you have reached the point where you have signed an application form, the following points are worth checking:

- Has a doctor organised a bed in the hospital and is the hospital expecting you?

- Have you arranged transport? It is your job to make sure that the patient gets to the hospital. The ambulance service should assist if needed. Check any local agreements.

- Have you made arrangements to protect any moveable property? Is there anyone to help with cancelling milk, etc.?

- You should leave a report at the hospital. This should include the patient's social circumstances and events leading up to the admission, including a note on alternatives that were not considered to be appropriate, plus any phone numbers, etc.

- Have you fully explained to the patient what is happening?

Note: The doctor providing the recommendation does not need to be section 12 approved and may not have previous acquaintance with the patient. This significantly reduces the safeguards for the patient and should be avoided if possible. It is important to remind the hospital to let the ASW know if the section is converted to a section 2 so that the ASW can inform the nearest relative as required by section 11(3).

SECTION 7 Application for guardianship (lasting up to six months and renewable)

(1) Are you of the opinion 'having regard to any wishes expressed by relatives of the patient or any other relevant circumstances' that your making an application would be necessary or proper?

(2) Is the patient at least 16 years old?

(3) Does your application specify at least one of the following forms of mental disorder *and* is this also common to *both* medical recommendations: mental illness, severe mental impairment, psychopathic disorder or mental impairment? If not, the application is invalid and a new one will have to be made.

(4) Have you got two medical recommendations which specify the mental disorder as above and state that this is 'of a nature or degree which warrants his reception into guardianship' and this is 'necessary in the interests of the welfare of the patient or for the protection of other persons'?

(5) Has one of the doctors had previous acquaintance with the patient? If not, every effort should be made to find one who has. If unsuccessful you must give your reasons near the bottom of Form 18.

(6) Has one doctor been approved as having special experience in psychiatry? See your local list of section 12 approved doctors.

(7) Have you seen the patient within the last 14 days and have the doctors personally examined the patient together or within five days of each other? (This means five clear days, i.e. one on first and the other on seventh is acceptable.)

(8) Have you consulted the nearest relative and checked that they have no objections to an application? If you have not, would you say that this was not reasonably practicable or would have involved unreasonable delay?

(9) Have you checked the validity of the medical recommendations (e.g. that they have been signed and that the form of disorder specified is appropriate for this section)? If not, and a mistake has been made, you could be notified and have to make a new application.

(10) Has the person you are naming as guardian (if not the local authority) given you a statement in writing that she/he is willing to act as guardian? Use Part II of Form 18.

(11) Are the dates of the signatures of both medical recommendations on or before the date of your application?

(12) You must now seek the approval of the social services department for the guardianship. You have 14 days from the date when the patient was last examined for one of the recommendations to forward the application to the responsible person in the social services department. This person will usually have been authorised by the social services committee to receive people into guardianship (unless you have to go to the committee itself – see local arrangements). There is no formal time limit on when the social services department then has to make a decision but any significant delay could lead to a complaint. You will almost certainly be asked to provide a detailed report on the patient and, where necessary, on the proposed guardian to help whoever has to make these decisions. Note that the person approving the guardian and agreeing to the guardianship would not have to be an approved social worker.

Forms required. Application on Form 18 (nearest relative would use Form 17. The social services department would then make its assessment of the appropriateness of guardianship, usually involving an approved social worker in this process).

Recommendations on Form 19 (joint) or Form 20.

Note that it is also possible for someone to be transferred into guardianship from detention in hospital using Form 25. Transfers from guardianship to detention under section 3 are also possible but require two medical recommendations and a fresh application from an ASW.

Appendix 2

Department of Health advice on the decision of the European Court of Human Rights in the case of *HL* v *UK* (the Bournewood case)

Purpose

1. This note is to provide further information for NHS bodies and local authorities about the implications of the judgment of European Court of Human Rights in the case of *HL* v *UK* (the Bournewood case).

It covers:

- a summary of the case and the key points of the judgment (paragraphs 2–29)
- steps to be taken by the Department of Health to develop proposals for new procedural safeguards (paragraphs 29–30)
- steps that might be taken in the interim by NHS bodies and local authorities pending the development of those new safeguards (paragraphs 32–8).

The case

2. The case concerned a man (Mr L) in his 40s with autism and learning disabilities. He is unable to speak and his level of understanding is limited. He is frequently agitated and has a history of self-harming behaviour. He lacks the capacity to consent or object to medical treatment.

3. For over 30 years Mr L was cared for in Bournewood Hospital ('the hospital'), a National Health Service trust hospital. In March 1994 he was discharged on a trial basis to paid carers with whom he successfully resided until July 1997.

4. In July 1997 Mr L was readmitted to Bournewood Hospital after an incident at a day-care centre when he became particularly agitated, hitting himself on the head with his fists and banging his head against the wall.

5. His consultant at the hospital considered detaining him under the Mental Health Act 1983 ('the 1983 Act') but concluded that that was not necessary as he was compliant and did not resist admission. Mr L was therefore admitted as an 'informal patient', in his own best interests under the common law doctrine of necessity. This was in line with standard practice. The consultant confirmed (in her submissions in the judicial review proceedings referred to below) that if the applicant had resisted admission, she would have detained him compulsorily under the 1983 Act as she was firmly of the view that he required in-patient treatment for his mental disorder. For clinical reasons, the

consultant advised Mr L's carers against visiting him initially, it appears on the basis that Mr L would think each time that he could go home with them.

6. Around September 1997, legal action was begun on Mr L's behalf to secure (amongst other things) his discharge from hospital. The action was unsuccessful in the High Court, but in December 1997 the Court of Appeal held that Mr L had been unlawfully detained. It also found that because of the Mental Health Act 1983 the common law doctrine of necessity could not be used to detain someone for treatment for mental disorder. Following this Mr L was formally detained under the Mental Health Act 1983, but was then discharged about six weeks later.

7. The Court of Appeal's judgment was subsequently overturned on 25 June 1998 by the House of Lords who found that Mr L had not been detained. The case was then taken to the European Court of Human Rights ('the European Court'). A hearing took place on 27 May 2003, and the Court's judgment was published on 5 October 2004. The Court found that there had been a violation of Articles 5(1) and 5(4) ('Right to liberty and security') of the European Convention on Human Rights. It held that these findings of violation themselves constituted 'just satisfaction' and therefore rejected Mr L's claim for damages. Mr L was awarded costs against the UK Government of around €27,000.

8. The full text of the judgment can be found on the European Court's website at *www.echr.coe.int/Eng/Judgments.htm* (Application number 45508/99).

The judgment and its implications

9. The case has important implications for NHS bodies, local authorities and other bodies involved in providing or arranging the care and treatment of people who lack capacity to consent to treatment in hospital and possibly in other residential settings as well. (For convenience such people are referred to in this note as 'incapacitated'.)

10. As public authorities, NHS bodies and local authorities are required by the Human Rights Act 1998 to act in way which is compatible with Convention rights (except to the extent that they are prevented from doing so by primary legislation which cannot be read in a way which is compatible with the Convention).

3 (a) Deprivation of liberty

11. The European Court found that Mr L had been deprived of his liberty within the meaning of Article 5(1) of the Convention which, in so far as is relevant, reads as follows: '1. Everyone has the right to liberty and security of person. No one shall be deprived of his liberty save in the following cases and in accordance with a procedure prescribed by law: (e) the lawful detention ... of persons of unsound mind'.

12. It is important to note that this judgment does not concern the treatment of incapacitated patients generally. It was concerned only with the question of deprivation of liberty of incapacitated persons.

13. The European Court made clear that the question of whether someone has, in fact, been deprived of liberty depends on the particular circumstances of the case. Specifically the Court said that: 'It is not disputed that in order to determine whether there has been a deprivation of liberty, the starting-point must be the specific situation of the individual concerned and account must be taken of a whole range of factors arising in a particular case such as the type, duration, effects and manner of implementation of the measure in question. The distinction between a deprivation of, and restriction upon,

liberty is merely one of degree or intensity and not one of nature or substance.' (paragraph 89 of the judgment)

14. The European Court's judgment does not, therefore, mean that incapacitated patients admitted to hospital or to care homes are automatically deprived of their liberty, even if staff would prevent them leaving unescorted for their own safety.

15. There must be particular factors which provide the 'degree' and 'intensity' to render the situation one of deprivation of liberty. The factors might relate, for example, to the type of care being provided, its duration, its effects and the way in which the admission came about.

16. In this case, the European Court said that 'the key factor in the present case [is] that the health care professionals treating and managing the applicant exercised complete and effective control over his care and movements': and, noting that Mr L had been resident with his carers for over three years, the Court went on to say that 'the clear intention of Dr M and the other relevant health care professionals [was] to exercise strict control over his assessment, treatment, contacts and, notably, movement and residence: the applicant would only be released from the hospital to the care of Mr and Mrs E as and when those professionals considered it appropriate'. (paragraph 91)

17. Accordingly, the Court found that 'the concrete situation was that the applicant was under continuous supervision and control and was not free to leave'. (paragraph 91)

18. The Court attached particular importance to the fact that Mr L had a settled home with his paid carers to which he was prevented from returning and that his contact with those carers was (to some extent) restricted by the staff of the hospital. The Court did not consider the issue of whether the ward was 'locked' or 'lockable' to be determinative.

(b) Lack of procedural safeguards

19. Unlike the Court of Appeal, the European Court did not find that Mr L's rights had been breached simply because he was admitted to hospital on the basis of the common law doctrine of necessity (i.e. in his 'best interests'), rather than under specific statutory provisions (e.g. the Mental Health Act 1983).

20. However, the Court did find that the absence of procedural safeguards surrounding his admission failed to protect him against 'arbitrary deprivations of liberty on grounds of necessity and, consequently, [failed] to comply with the essential purpose of Article 5(1) of the Convention'.

21. In this latter respect, the European Court was clearly influenced by the 'lack of any fixed procedural rules by which the admission and detention of compliant incapacitated persons is conducted' when contrasted with 'the extensive network of safeguards applicable to psychiatric committals covered by the [Mental Health Act] 1983'. The Court said, 'In particular and most obviously, the Court notes the lack of any formalised admission procedures which indicate who can propose admission, for what reasons and on the basis of what kind of medical and other assessments and conclusions. There is no requirement to fix the exact purpose of admission (for example, for assessment or for treatment) and, consistently, no limits in terms of time, treatment or care attach to that admission. Nor is there any specific provision requiring a continuing clinical assessment of the persistence of a disorder warranting detention.' (paragraph 120)

22. The European Court also said, 'the nomination of a representative of a patient who could make certain objections and applications on his or her behalf is a procedural protection accorded to those committed involuntarily under the 1983 Act and which would be of equal importance for patients who are legally incapacitated and have, as in the present case, extremely limited communication abilities' (para. 120) by which it presumably had in mind the role of nearest relative under the Mental Health Act 1983.

23. Above all, although it did not question their good faith, the Court seems to have been concerned that the hospital's health care professionals were able to assume 'full control of the liberty and treatment of a vulnerable incapacitated individual solely on the basis of their own clinical assessments completed as and when they considered fit' (paragraph 121).

24. The Court did not say that Mr L should have been formally detained under the Mental Health Act 1983. Nor, in the government's view, does the judgment mean that procedural safeguards for people in Mr L's position must be identical to those for patients detained under the Mental Health Act 1983. Indeed, the Court noted the 'Government's understandable concern ... to avoid the full, formal and inflexible impact of the 1983 Act.'

25. However, the government accepts that to avoid further violations of Article 5(1) new procedural safeguards are required for patients who are not formally detained, but who are, in effect, deprived of their liberty in their best interests under the common law doctrine of necessity.

(c) Breach of Article 5(4)

26. The European Court also found a violation of Mr L's rights under Article 5(4) of the Convention, which reads as follows: 'Everyone who is deprived of his liberty by arrest or detention shall be entitled to take proceedings by which the lawfulness of his detention shall be decided speedily by a court and his release ordered if the detention is not lawful.'

27. The European Court said that Article 5(4) gives 'the right to an individual deprived of his liberty to have the lawfulness of that detention reviewed by a court in the light, not only of domestic law requirements, but also of the text of the Convention, the general principles embodied therein and the aim of the restrictions permitted by paragraph 1: the scheme of Article 5 implies that the notion of "lawfulness" should have the same significance in paragraphs 1 (e) and 4 [of Article 5] in relation to the same deprivation of liberty. This does not guarantee a right to review of such scope as to empower the court on all aspects of the case or to substitute its own discretion for that of the decision-making authority. The review should, however, be wide enough to bear on those conditions which are essential for the lawful detention of a person, in this case, on the ground of unsoundness of mind.'

28. The European Court also found that, at the time (in 1997 and 1998), neither judicial review nor any other legal remedy was sufficient to guarantee a review of this nature.

29. The government's view is that action has already been taken in the Human Rights Act 1998 to prevent further violations of Article 5(4).[1]

---

1 The government is considering whether any further action is needed in the light of the Court of Appeal's judgement of 3 December in the case of *R (MH)* v *Secretary of State for Health*, which concerned the Mental Health Act 1983.

Next steps

(a) Proposals for new procedural safeguards

30. As set out above, the government accepts that to avoid further violations of Article 5(1) additional procedural safeguards are required for incapacitated patients who are not formally detained, but who are, in effect, deprived of their liberty.

31. It will therefore bring forward proposals for appropriate new safeguards as soon as possible. Before doing so, it will consult with interested parties, including representative groups, the NHS and local authorities. Its aim is to ensure that there are procedural safeguards which are effective, proportionate and deliverable in practice.

(b) Steps that might be taken in the interim by NHS bodies and local authorities

32. Until these safeguards are established in law, the effect of the judgment is that it would be unlawful for an NHS body or a local authority (without the prior authorisation of the High Court) to arrange or provide care or treatment for an incapacitated patient in a way that amounted to deprivation of liberty within the meaning of article 5 of the Convention, unless the patient were detained under the Mental Health Act 1983.

33. Nonetheless, the NHS and local authorities will need to continue to provide care and treatment for incapacitated patients, and it is important that neither the safety of those patients nor the quality of the care they receive is jeopardised during the interim period.

34. Pending the development of new safeguards described above, NHS bodies and local authorities will want to consider what steps they can take in the short term to protect incapacitated people against the risk of arbitrary deprivation of liberty and minimise the risk of further successful legal challenges.

35. The government suggests that NHS bodies and local authorities will want to ensure they have systems in place so that when making arrangements to provide care to an incapacitated person which involves a restriction on the liberty of that person consideration is given to whether what they are proposing amounts in practice to a deprivation of that person's liberty within the meaning of article 5 of the Convention, taking into account the range of factors identified by the Court as described in paragraphs 12 to 19 above. The same question will need to be asked when reviewing the circumstances of those people who they have already placed who may, in practice, be deprived of their liberty.

36. If patients are considered to be deprived of their liberty (or at risk of it), consideration should always be given to alternatives to ensure that they get adequate care but which falls short of deprivation of liberty. In particular, authorities will want wherever possible to avoid situations in which professionals may be said to take 'full and effective control' over patients' care and liberty.

37. Elements of good practice which are likely to assist in this, and in avoiding the risk of legal challenge, may include:

   - Ensuring that decisions are taken (and reviewed) in a structured way, which includes safeguards against arbitrary deprivation of liberty. There should, for example, be a proper assessment of whether the patient lacks capacity to decide whether or not to accept the care proposed, and that decision should taken on the basis of proper medical advice by a person properly equipped to make the judgement.

   - Effective, documented care planning (including the Care Programme Approach where relevant) for such patients, including appropriate and documented involvement of family, friends, carers (both paid and unpaid) and others interested in their welfare.

- Ensuring that alternatives to admission to hospital or residential care are considered and that any restrictions placed on the patient while in hospital or residential care should be kept to the minimum necessary in all the circumstances of their case.

- Ensuring appropriate information is given to patients themselves and to family, friends and carers. This would include information about the purpose and reasons for the patient's admission, proposals to review the care plan and the outcome of such reviews, and the way in which they can challenge decisions (e.g. through the relevant complaints procedure). The involvement of local advocacy services where these are available could be encouraged to support patients and their families, friends and carers.

- Taking proper steps to help patients retain contact with family, friends, carers, with proper consideration given to the views of those people. If, exceptionally, there are good clinical reasons why that is not in the patient's best interests, those reasons should be properly documented and explained to the people they affect – ensuring both the assessment of capacity and the care plan are kept under review. It may well be helpful to include an independent element in the review. Depending on the circumstances, this might be achieved by involvement of social work or community health staff, or by seeking a second medical (or other appropriate clinical) opinion either from within the organisation or elsewhere. Such a second opinion will be particularly important where family members, carers or friends do not agree with the authority's decisions. But even where there is no dispute an authority must ensure its decision making stands up to scrutiny.

38. If it is concluded that there is no way of providing appropriate care which does not amount to deprivation of liberty, then consideration will have to be given to using the formal powers of detention in the Mental Health Act 1983. However, it is important to remember that:

- Nothing in the judgment changes the requirements in the Mental Health Act which must be met before patients can be detained. It should not therefore be assumed that all patients who are to be subject to restrictions which may amount to deprivation of liberty can be detained under the Act. (For example, it would be unlawful to detain patients under the Act if their mental disorder does not warrant detention in hospital, although reception into guardianship under the Act might be appropriate in some cases.)

- There are dangers in using the Act simply to be 'on the safe side'. Although it provides procedural safeguards, the use of the Mental Health Act will not necessarily be welcomed by patients themselves or by their family, friends or carers, given the 'stigma' that is often (wrongly) perceived to attach to it. Moreover, a significant increase in the use of the Mental Health Act will inevitably put considerable further pressure on local authority approved social workers, the availability of second opinion appointed doctors (SOADs) and on the operation of Mental Health Review Tribunals (MHRT).

Further information

39. For inquiries about this note, please write to the Bournewood Team, Room 315, Department of Health, Wellington House, 133-155 Waterloo Road, London SE1 8UG, or via *MBBournewood.Advice@dh.gsi.gov.uk*.

Please note, however, that the Department cannot provide legal advice to individual NHS bodies, local authorities, or independent providers. They must take their own legal advice.

(Department of Health 10 December 2004)

Appendix 3

Mental Health Act 1983: arrangement of sections

IV **Consent to treatment**

s56   patients to whom Part IV applies

s57   treatment requiring consent and a second opinion

s58   treatment requiring consent or a second opinion

s62   urgent treatment

s63   treatment not requiring consent

V **Mental Health Review Tribunals**

s65   Mental Health Review Tribunals

s72   powers of tribunals

VI **Removal and return of patients within UK, etc.**

VII **Management of property and affairs of patients**

s93   judicial authorities and Court of Protection

VIII **Miscellaneous functions of local authorities and Secretary of State**

s114   appointment of approved social workers

s115   powers of entry and inspection

s117   after-care

IX **Offences**

s129   obstruction

s130   prosecutions by local authorities

X **Miscellaneous and supplementary**

s131   informal admission of patients

s135   warrant to search for and remove patients

s136   mentally disordered persons found in public places

s137   provisions as to custody, conveyance and detention

s139   protection for acts done in pursuance of this Act

s145   interpretation (includes definition of ASW

(see various regulations, rules, circulars and the Code of Practice)

References

Age Concern (1986) *The Law and Vulnerable Elderly People*, Age Concern.

Barnes, M. *et al.* (1990) *Sectioned; Social Services and 1983 Mental Health Act*, Routledge.

Bean, P. T. *et al.* (1991) *Out of Harm's Way*, MIND.

Brayne, H., Martin, G. and **Carr, H.** (2005) *Law For Social Workers* (ninth edition), Oxford University Press.

CCETSW Paper (2000) *Assuring Quality for Mental Health Social Work*, CCETSW.

Department of Health/Home Office (1992) *Review of Health and Social Services for Mentally Disordered Offenders and Others Requiring Similar Services. Final Summary Report*, Cmnd 2088, HMSO.

Department of Health and Scottish Office (1991) *Care Management and Assessment: Practitioners' Guide*, HMSO.

Department of Health and Welsh Office (1997) *Mental Health Act 1983*, Code of Practice, HMSO.

Department of Health (1997) Who Decides? *Making Decisions on Behalf of Mentally Incapacitated Adults*, HMSO.

Department of Health (1999) *Reform of the Mental Health Act 1983*, The Stationery Office.

DHSS (1975a) *Better Services for the Mentally Ill*, Cmnd 6233, HMSO.

DHSS (1975b) *Report of Committee on Mentally Abnormal Offenders* (the Butler Report), Cmnd 6244, TSO.

DHSS (1976) *Review of the Mental Health Act 1959,* HMSO.

DHSS (1978) *Review of the Mental Health Act 1959*, Cmnd 7230, HMSO.

DHSS (1981) *Reforming Mental Health Legislation*, Cmnd 8405, HMSO

DHSS (1988) *Community Care: AgendaforAction* (the Griffiths Report), HMSO

DHSS (1997) *Memorandum to the Mental Health Act 1983*, The Stationery Office.

Eldergill, A. (1988) *Mental Health Review Tribunals*, Sweet and Maxwell.

Fernando, S. (ed.) (1995) *Mental Health in a Multi-Ethnic Society*, Routledge.

Franklin, D. *et al* (2000) Consultant psychiatrists' experiences of using supervised discharge: results of a national survey. Psychiatric Bulletin, 24, 412-15.

Gelder, M., Gath, D. and **Mayou, R.** (1989) *Oxford Textbook of Psychiatry* (second edition), Oxford University Press.

Goldberg, D. and **Huxley, P.** (1992) *Common Mental Disorders: A Bio-social Model*, Tavistock/Routledge.

Gostin, L. (1975) *A Human Condition*, Vol. 1, MIND.

Gostin, L. (1977) *A Human Condition*, Vol. 2, MIND.

Gostin, L. and **Fennell, P.** (1992) *Mental Health: Tribunal Procedure*, Longman.

Harbour, A. and **Ayotte, W.** (1995) *Mental Health Handbook: A Guide to the Law Affecting Children and Young People* (second edition), The Children's Legal Centre.

Hoggett, B. (1996) *Mental Health Law* (fourth edition), Sweet and Maxwell.

Home Office (2003) *Police and Criminal Evidence Act 1984: Codes of Practice*, HMSO.

House of Lords and House of Commons (2005) Joint Committee on the Draft Mental Health Bill, HL Paper 79-1, TSO.

Jones, R. (ed.) (2004) *Mental Health Act Manual* (ninth edition), Sweet and Maxwell.

This contains:

Mental Health Act 1983; DoH and Welsh Office (1999) *Mental Health Act 1983: Code of Practice*; MH Review Tribunal Rules 1983; Mental Health (Hospital, Guardianship and Consent to Treatment) Regulations 1983; as well as circulars and guidance.

Jones' *Manual* is extracted from the looseleaf work *The Encyclopaedia of Social Services and Child Care Law* (2004). This four-volume work is available for reference in some libraries.

Law Commission (1991) *Mentally Incapacitated Adults and Decision-Making. An Overview.* Consultation Paper No. 119, HMSO.

Law Commission (1995) *Mental Incapacity*. Law Com. No. 231.

Leff, J. and **Vaughn, C.** (1985) *Expressed Emotion in Families*, Guilford.

Mental Health Act Commission (1999) Eighth Biennial Report 1997–1999, The Stationery Office.

Montgomery, J. (2002) *Health Care Law*, Oxford University Press.

Peay, J. (1989) *Tribunals on Trial: Study of Decision Making under the MH Act 1983*, Oxford University Press.

Peay, J. (2003) *Decisions and Dilemmas: Working With Mental Health Law*, Hart.

Puri, B., Brown, R., McKee, H. and **Treasaden, I.** (2005) *Mental Health Law*, Hodder Arnold.

Rogers, A. and **Faulkner, A.** (1987) *A Place of Safety: MIND's research into police referrals to the psychiatric services*, MIND.

Sainsbury Centre (2000) Briefing 12. *An Executive Briefing on the implications of the Human Rights Act 1998 for Mental Health Services*, The Sainsbury Centre for Mental Health.

Swanson et al. (1990) *Hospital and Community Psychiatry*, 41, 761–70.

Wadham, J., Mountfield, H. and **Edmundson, A.** (2003) *Human Rights Act 1998* (third edition), Oxford University Press.

Wallington, P. and **Lee, R.** (2005) *Statutes on Public Law and Human Rights* (fifteenth edition), Oxford University Press.

West Midlands RHA (1991) The Report of the Panel of Inquiry Appointed to Investigate the Case of Kim Kirkman, West Midlands RHA.

Zander, M. (1995) *The Police and Criminal Evidence Act 1984* (third edition), Sweet and Maxwell.

Some useful websites

Department of Health	**www.doh.gov.uk**
Mental Health Act Commission	**www.mhac.org.uk**
Mental health law (IMHAP site)	**www.markwalton.net**

The IMHAP website has a number of links to other websites with useful material on mental health law and so is probably the best starting point.

Index